# Selected Titles in This Series

38  **Rebecca N. Wright and Peter G. Neumann, Editors,** Network Threats
37  **Boris Mirkin, F. R. McMorris, Fred S. Roberts, and Andrey Rzhetsky, Editors,** Mathematical Hierarchies and Biology
36  **Joseph G. Rosenstein, Deborah S. Franzblau, and Fred S. Roberts, Editors,** Discrete Mathematics in the Schools
35  **Dingzhu Du, Jun Gu, and Panos M. Pardalos, Editors,** Satisfiability Problem: Theory and Applications
34  **Nathaniel Dean, Editor,** African Americans in Mathematics
33  **Ravi B. Boppana and James F. Lynch, Editors,** Logic and random structures
32  **Jean-Charles Grégoire, Gerard J. Holzmann, and Doron A. Peled, Editors,** The SPIN verification system
31  **Neil Immerman and Phokion G. Kolaitis, Editors,** Descriptive complexity and finite models
30  **Sandeep N. Bhatt, Editor,** Parallel Algorithms: Third DIMACS Implementation Challenge
29  **Doron A. Peled, Vaughan R. Pratt, and Gerard J. Holzmann, Editors,** Partial Order Methods in Verification
28  **Larry Finkelstein and William M. Kantor, Editors,** Groups and Computation II
27  **Richard J. Lipton and Eric B. Baum, Editors,** DNA Based Computers
26  **David S. Johnson and Michael A. Trick, Editors,** Cliques, Coloring, and Satisfiability: Second DIMACS Implementation Challenge
25  **Gilbert Baumslag, David Epstein, Robert Gilman, Hamish Short, and Charles Sims, Editors,** Geometric and Computational Perspectives on Infinite Groups
24  **Louis J. Billera, Curtis Greene, Rodica Simion, and Richard P. Stanley, Editors,** Formal Power Series and Algebraic Combinatorics/Séries formelles et combinatoire algébrique, 1994
23  **Panos M. Pardalos, David I. Shalloway, and Guoliang Xue, Editors,** Global Minimization of Nonconvex Energy Functions: Molecular Conformation and Protein Folding
22  **Panos M. Pardalos, Mauricio G. C. Resende, and K. G. Ramakrishnan, Editors,** Parallel Processing of Discrete Optimization Problems
21  **D. Frank Hsu, Arnold L. Rosenberg, and Dominique Sotteau, Editors,** Interconnection Networks and Mapping and Scheduling Parallel Computations
20  **William Cook, László Lovász, and Paul Seymour, Editors,** Combinatorial Optimization
19  **Ingemar J. Cox, Pierre Hansen, and Bela Julesz, Editors,** Partitioning Data Sets
18  **Guy E. Blelloch, K. Mani Chandy, and Suresh Jagannathan, Editors,** Specification of Parallel Algorithms
17  **Eric Sven Ristad, Editor,** Language Computations
16  **Panos M. Pardalos and Henry Wolkowicz, Editors,** Quadratic Assignment and Related Problems
15  **Nathaniel Dean and Gregory E. Shannon, Editors,** Computational Support for Discrete Mathematics
14  **Robert Calderbank, G. David Forney, Jr., and Nader Moayeri, Editors,** Coding and Quantization: DIMACS/IEEE Workshop
13  **Jin-Yi Cai, Editor,** Advances in Computational Complexity Theory
12  **David S. Johnson and Catherine C. McGeoch, Editors,** Network Flows and Matching: First DIMACS Implementation Challenge
11  **Larry Finkelstein and William M. Kantor, Editors,** Groups and Computation
10  **Joel Friedman, Editor,** Expanding Graphs

*(Continued in the back of this publication)*

# Network Threats

# DIMACS
Series in Discrete Mathematics
and Theoretical Computer Science

Volume 38

## Network Threats

DIMACS Workshop
December 2–4, 1996

Rebecca N. Wright
Peter G. Neumann
Editors

NSF Science and Technology Center
in Discrete Mathematics and Theoretical Computer Science
A consortium of Rutgers University, Princeton University,
AT&T Labs, Bell Labs, and Bellcore

**American Mathematical Society**

The Workshop on "Network Threats", held in December 1996, was part of the DIMACS 1996–1997 Special Year on Networks.

1991 *Mathematics Subject Classification.* Primary 68–06, 68M10, 94B12; Secondary 68P25, 94A60, 68N99.

---

**Library of Congress Cataloging-in-Publication Data**
Network threats : DIMACS workshop, December 1996 / Rebecca N. Wright, Peter G. Neumann, editors.
   p. cm. — (DIMACS series in discrete mathematics and theoretical computer science)
   Includes bibliographical references.
   ISBN 0-8218-0832-X (alk. paper)
   1. Computer networks—Congresses.  I. Wright, Rebecca N., 1967– .  II. Neumann, Peter, 1932– .  III. Series.
TK5105.5.N4668  1997
004.6—dc21                                                                                           97-30683
                                                                                                          CIP

---

**Copying and reprinting.** Material in this book may be reproduced by any means for educational and scientific purposes without fee or permission with the exception of reproduction by services that collect fees for delivery of documents and provided that the customary acknowledgment of the source is given. This consent does not extend to other kinds of copying for general distribution, for advertising or promotional purposes, or for resale. Requests for permission for commercial use of material should be addressed to the Assistant to the Publisher, American Mathematical Society, P. O. Box 6248, Providence, Rhode Island 02940-6248. Requests can also be made by e-mail to reprint-permission@ams.org.
   Excluded from these provisions is material in articles for which the author holds copyright. In such cases, requests for permission to use or reprint should be addressed directly to the author(s). (Copyright ownership is indicated in the notice in the lower right-hand corner of the first page of each article.)

© 1998 by the American Mathematical Society. All rights reserved.
The American Mathematical Society retains all rights
except those granted to the United States Government.
Printed in the United States of America.

∞ The paper used in this book is acid-free and falls within the guidelines
established to ensure permanence and durability.
Visit the AMS home page at URL: http://www.ams.org/

10 9 8 7 6 5 4 3 2 1     03 02 01 00 99 98

# Contents

| | |
|---|---|
| Foreword | ix |
| Preface | xi |
| A representation of protocol attacks for risk assessment<br>CATHERINE MEADOWS | 1 |
| Verifying privacy enchanced mail functions with higher order logic<br>DAN ZHOU AND SHIU-KAI CHIN | 11 |
| Cryptanalysis of RSA-type cryptosystems: A visit<br>MARC JOYE AND JEAN-JACQUES QUISQUATER | 21 |
| Information leakage in encrypted key exchange<br>SARVAR PATEL | 33 |
| Observed weaknesses in security dynamics' client/server protocol<br>ADAM SHOSTACK | 41 |
| Web security: A high level view<br>DREW DEAN | 55 |
| Flexible, extensible Java security using digital signatures<br>DAN S. WALLACH, JIM A. ROSKIND, AND EDWARD W. FELTEN | 59 |
| Trust and security: A new look at the Byzantine generals problem<br>MIKE BURMESTER, YVO DESMEDT, AND GREGORY KABATIANSKI | 75 |
| Channels: Avoiding unwanted electronic mail<br>ROBERT J. HALL | 85 |
| Demonstration of hacker techniques<br>CYNTHIA CULLEN | 103 |

# Foreword

The Workshop on "Network Threats" held in December 1996 was part of DIMACS 1996–1997 Special Year on Networks. We would like to express our appreciation to Rebecca Wright of AT&T and Peter Neumann of SRI International for their efforts editing this volume of papers that brings these talks on emerging issues in network security to a wider audience. We also extend our thanks to Rebecca Wright, Peter Neumann and Steven Bellovin of AT&T for their efforts in organizing the successful workshop where these papers appear in preliminary talks.

The workshop was part of DIMACS' Special Year on Networks which is examining security, applications, control and design of networks. The special year encouraged practitioners to communicate research problems in these areas to theorists and had a goal of fostering communication between these groups. We also extend our thanks to Stuart Haber of Surety Technologies, David S. Johnson of AT&T, and Mihalis Yannakakis of Bell Labs for their time and efforts as organizers of the special year.

DIMACS gratefully acknowledges the generous support that makes these programs possible. The National Science Foundation, through its Science and Technology Center program, the New Jersey Commission on Science and Technology, DIMACS' partners at Rutgers, Princeton, AT&T Labs, Bell Labs, and Bellcore generously supported the special year.

> Fred S. Roberts
> Director
>
> Bernard Chazelle
> Co-Director for Princeton
>
> Stephen R. Mahaney
> Associate Director for Research

# Preface

In December 1996, a three-day workshop on Network Threats was held at DIMACS in New Brunswick, New Jersey, as part of a special year on Networks. This workshop brought together around one hundred computer science researchers, both theorists and practitioners, working in the area of network security, in an informal setting. The goal of the workshop was to foster discussion on topics such as attacks on network security, prevention and detection of attacks, modeling threat, threats to individual privacy, risk management, and formal methods of security analysis.

As the use of computer networks, and in particular the Internet, has increased, so has the potential threat to security. In the last several years, we have seen numerous security-related attacks on Java, Netscape Navigator, Internet Explorer, Web servers (various U.S. Websites were penetrated, including the CIA, Department of Justice, U.S. Air Force, and NASA), Microsoft Word (viruses), operating systems, cryptographic implementations (with a remarkable assortment of conceptual attacks and exhaustive key searches), and the Internet protocols. Several serious denial-of-service attacks were mounted against commercial Internet service providers. New protocols and systems for electronic commerce, secure financial transactions, and other applications are being introduced, and are being deployed quickly, and on a large scale. However, they tend to be flawed as well.

"Network Threats" covers a wide and diverse range of topics, as the collection of papers presented here demonstrates. More and more of our interactions and transactions are taking place electronically, in a networked environment. The increased functionality this brings is desirable, but it brings with it increased threat to confidentiality, privacy, integrity, and availability. This volume includes things that have gone wrong in the past, along with lessons learned. It also contains several new attacks and weaknesses, both in protocols and in underlying cryptographic methods, and formal analysis methods to identify, quantify, and combat security threats. And of course, we'll hear about the Internet, the Web, and Java.

The papers presented in this volume are unrefereed. Indeed, many of them describe preliminary results and ongoing work. It is our hope and expectation that many of them will be published in referreed journals in their final form. Following is a brief summary of each included paper.

In order to determine whether a system is secure, it is first necessary to understand the potential risks to the system and whether they may make the system insecure. Formal methods can be helpful both in assessing risk and in proving various security properties. In "A Representation of Protocol Attacks for Risk Assessment", Catherine Meadows presents a graphical representation of possible

© 1998 AT&T Corp.

intrusion attacks that can be used to clarify the risks of using a particular protocol. In "Verifying Privacy Enhanced Mail Functions with Higher Order Logic", Dan Zhou and Shiu-Kai Chin use HOL (Higher Order Logic) to prove certain security properties about PEM (Privacy Enhanced Mail).

Because any system is only as secure as its weakest link, threats are multiplied as systems become more complex and diverse. Attacks can be directed at the underlying cryptography, at the protocols that use cryptography to perform functions such key exchange and authentication, or at the way in which such protocols are implemented and administered in a particular system. "Cryptanalysis of RSA-type Cryptosystems: A Visit", by Marc Joye and Jean-Jacques Quisquater, surveys a number of attacks on certain RSA-type implementations. In addition, they present some guidelines for choosing the most appropriate cryptosystem for particular applications. In "Information Leakage in Encrypted Key Exchange", Sarvar Patel describes an attack on the Encrypted Key Exchange (EKE) protocol of Bellovin and Merritt, and also describes a modification to EKE that is not subject to such attacks. "Observed Weaknesses in Security Dynamics' Client/Server Protocol", by Adam Shostack, describes an attack on some versions of Security Dynamics' ACE protocol, a protocol widely used to perform authentication using a small handheld card to provide better security for remote access than a password-based system. The attack reduces the security of the ACE protocol to that of a password-based system. In "Web Security: A High Level View", Drew Dean gives an overview of many implementation and architectural problems that threaten the security of the World Wide Web.

The study of network threats also involves the finding of new, better solutions to make less vulnerable systems. "Flexible, Extensible Java Security Using Digital Signatures", by Dan S. Wallach, Jim A. Roskind, and Edward W. Felten, describes a method for using digital signatures to allow Java programs to achieve a user-customizable balance between functionality and security. Their system will be implemented as part of Netscape Navigator 4.0. In "Trust and Security: A New Look at the Byzantine Generals Problem", Mike Burmester, Yvo Desmedt, and Gregory Kabatianski explore the importance of knowing who trusts whom in a communication network. They address the problem of end-to-end authentication using a primitive of link authentication, and show that while the problem is solvable if the end points know the trust relationships in the network, it may not be otherwise. In "Channels: Avoiding Unwanted Electronic Mail", Robert J. Hall describes a solution to the so-called spamming problem. The Channels system allows a user to easily create and manage different user e-mail addresses. E-mail will then, depending on the attributes of the address, be presented to the user differently: for example, as high priority, as low priority, or not at all.

As in all battles, it is important in the battle of network security to know one's enemy. In "Demonstration of Hacker Techniques", Cynthia Cullen describes several tools that have historically been used by the hacker community.

In addition to the papers printed here, the Network Threats workshop program had several talks for which no paper is available for inclusion in this volume.

Among those was the keynote talk, given by Peter Neumann. That talk presented a system-oriented view of risks in computer-communication networks, from a holistic perspective. He addressed risks relating to security, reliability, and availability (among others) in a wide range of environments—including not just the Internet and WWW, but also power transmission and distribution, public switched communications networks, air-traffic control, and other critical systems—and how those risks are interrelated. The talk considered what we have or have not learned in the past, and where the major remaining problems are. It explored common problems and potential approaches, concerning both maliciously and accidentally caused incidents, and consider how to develop a constructive course of action for the future. His cumulative Illustrative Risks summary (ftp://ftp.csl.sri.com/pub/illustrative.PS) was given to all workshop participants, providing many examples of the pervasiveness of the risks. Additional background and pointers can be found at his Web site (http://www.csl.sri.com/neumann.html).

Denial-of-service attacks are generally believed by the security community to be easy to carry out and impossible to prevent. Until recently, however, no large scale denial-of-service attacks had been carried out. In his invited talk, "Understanding and Defending Against SYN Attacks", Alexis Rosen, owner of PANIX/Public Access Networks Corporation, spoke about their recent experience with a denial of service attack carried out on the PANIX network. The attack involved flooding the network with SYN packets, each initiating a connection request. Rosen described the measures, both technical and procedural, that PANIX took first to determine that they were under attack, and then to defend against it.

Ed Felten spoke about spoofing attacks on the Web. These attacks are not technical attacks on Web or Internet protocols themselves, but rather social engineering attacks with a technical spin. For example, a Java program can pop up a legitimate-looking dialog box asking for a password or other sensitive information, fooling the user into giving this information. A more sophisticated example is "mirroring" the entire Web, spoofing a user into believing she is looking at the real Web, when in fact she is looking at an attacker's mirrored, and possibly modified, copy. Such attacks demonstrate the need for unspoofable content. They also demonstrate the security difficulties that arise due to the involvement of people, who may not understand the systems they are using well enough to recognize such attacks when they occur. Several related talks were given, two of which are represented in this volume: "Web Security: A High Level View", by Drew Dean and "Flexible, Extensible Java Security Using Digital Signatures", by Dan S. Wallach, Jim A. Roskind, and Edward W. Felten. These talks were followed by a discussion "Webware: Can it be secured?", with panelists Steve Bellovin, Drew Dean, Ed Felten, Avi Rubin, and Dan Wallach. The discussion repeatedly touched on the conflict between on one hand, the desire of both software developers and consumers for quick software releases incorporating more capabilities and, on the other hand, the need for careful design and implementation to address security concerns.

In conclusion, the workshop was a very timely assessment of the difficulty and breadth of the fundamental problem of avoiding or minimizing network threats. A broad interdisciplinary system-oriented approach is absolutely essential, encompassing requirements, specifications, protocols, algorithms, implementation, and development strategy in real-world applications, while encompassing security, reliability, fault tolerance, and even real-time performance considerations. In the setting of discussing work in progress, the participants reflected those needs in their backgrounds and interests, and have given us considerable hope that future collaborations and new research directions may emerge from this workshop.

We would like to extend our thanks to DIMACS and the organizers of the Special Year on Networks for making the Network Threats workshop possible. We also thank all the authors, invited speakers, and other participants of the workshop, as well as our co-organizer Steve Bellovin, for making it a productive and enjoyable experience.

REBECCA N. WRIGHT
Florham Park, New Jersey

PETER G. NEUMANN
Menlo Park, California

June 1997

DIMACS Series in Discrete Mathematics
and Theoretical Computer Science
Volume **38**, 1998

# A Representation of Protocol Attacks for Risk Assessment

## Catherine Meadows

ABSTRACT. This paper describes a visual means of representing protocol attacks so that the risks involved in using the protocol are made clearer. This is done by dividing an attack into stages, and using visual means of representing the relationship between the stages and the difficulty of each stage. An outline of a taxonomy of stages for protocol attacks is provided, and several examples are presented.

### Introduction

Measuring the security risks to which a system is subject is a notoriously difficult proposition. Relative strengths of different kinds of protection mechanisms are hard to evaluate, and much depends upon hard to measure variables such as motivation of intruders, the amount of resources an intruder has available, the kinds of uses to which the system will be put, and the type of environment in which the system operates. The problem becomes even more difficult when the system is one with a known vulnerability. Here the risk of using the system must be decided upon by weighing the difficulty of exploiting the vulnerability, the intruder's resources, the payoff to the intruder of exploiting the vulnerability, and the presence of other vulnerabilities in the system that may or may not be easier to exploit.

Although the risk of using systems with known vulnerabilities is hard to quantify, it is a problem that faces us daily. Even when a system is itself secure, it may have to interact with systems with known vulnerabilities. Indeed, this is true for any system hooked up to the Internet. What risk is involved for a system in allowing these systems access to its resources, and what services can it allow these systems to perform for it with a reasonable degree of assurance that it is not courting disaster?

Although it may not be possible to quantify exactly the degree of risk posed by a vulnerability, it is still possible to develop techniques that allow one to compare risks posed by different vulnerabilities. One such technique is to outline the procedure (or *attack*) that an intruder would have to go through in order to take advantage of the vulnerability. If the procedure can be broken down into a set of well-defined components, then it may be possible to evaluate, or at least compare, the difficulty of executing each component and the payoffs gained by executing it. This understanding may lead us to a greater understanding of the difficulty and payoffs involved in the attack as a whole.

This approach of assessing risk in terms of possible attacks on a system has been used in a number of different risk assessment models. For example, the ANSSR system [**BCK90**] includes a scenario-based analysis techniques in which attack scenarios are collected and each is assigned a risk level. A scenario is modeled as a sequence of events. The likelihood of a scenario is calculated in terms of

---

1991 *Mathematics Subject Classification.* Primary 54C40, 14E20; Secondary 46E25, 20C20.
This work was supported by the Office of Naval Research.

© 1998 American Mathematical Society

the probabilities of a scenario being attempted and of a scenario succeeding if it is attempted. The probability of a scenario succeeding is computed in terms of the probability of each event succeeding if the previous events have succeeded. Similarly, in [**LBF**$^+$**93**] Littlewood et al. discuss the possibility in modeling security breaches in terms of atomic events, such as guessing a password. They point out that, in general, one would expect the events used to mount a security breach would have a descending rate of failure as the breach progressed. Another similar approach is taken by Dacier and Deswarte [**DD94, Dac94**], in which attacks are modeled in terms of *privilege graphs*, in which the nodes are collections or privileges and the edges represent means of acquiring privileges, illicitly or otherwise. Numbers representing the difficulty of a means of acquiring privileges can be assigned to each edge. A tool for risk assessment has been built that makes use of privilege graphs to discover and display possible attacks [**DDK96, ODK97**].

The approach taken in this paper is similar to those described above, but there are important differences. The main difference is that we do not assign numerical values to the likelyhood of atomic events. Instead, we rely upon a visual representation of an attack and the difficulty of its various stages to help give the user an intuitive feeling for the difficulty of an attack. Our visual representation of attacks is similar to that of Dacier and Deswarte, except that, since we are more interested in representing the attack process than in discovering possible attacks, our nodes are stages of the attack process itself rather than collections of privileges.

The approach we take is as follows. An attack is divided into a number of stages, each of which consists of a sequence of atomic events. One stage may enable another in the sense that the second stage cannot complete until the first does. We also develop a taxonomy of stages in terms of various features that may affect the difficulty of completing a stage successfully. The difficulty of successfully completing a stage, and the likelyhood of its being attempted, is estimated on the basis of its place in the taxonomy. This can be used to give an estimate or rough idea of the difficulty of that attack as a whole. Finally, we develop a graphical means of representing attacks where the stages and the relationships between them are emphasized. Our intent is to give a simple easy-to-read representation that can be used to give help in comparing the severity and likelyhood of different attacks, even when exact numeric figures are absent.

In the remainder of the paper, we outline our basic procedure for describing attacks and representing them graphically. We also show how our techniques would work on an example application: cryptographic protocols.

## Definitions

In this section we give an informal definition of an attack and other notions asscated with it.

**Definition**: We define an *attack* to be a sequence of actions on the part of an intruder that allows him or her to either gain unauthorized use of a resource or to prevent another party from making legitimate use of a resource.

We note that we use the word "resource" in a very broad sense. For example, a resource can be information (such as a cryptographic key), or it can be money (such as in a banking or electronic cash protocol), or it can be the ability to execute programs.

Attacks may proceed in stages, such that the successful completion of one stage makes possible the successful completion of the second stage, possibly more than once. For an example, in the Needham-Schroeder protocol [**NS78**], compromise of an old session key and knowledge of the messages that were passed when that key was distributed allows an intruder to pass of that key as a current one repeatedly [**DS81**]. We can consider the first stage to be that in which the protocol is executed, the second stage to be that in which the intruder records the messages used in distributing the key, and the third state to be that in which the key is compromised. The fourth stage is that in which the intruder passes off the old key as a new one. That stage can be executed repeatedly after the first stage is complete. We define the notion of stage more precisely below.

**Definition**: We define a *stage* of an attack to be a subsequence of an attack. We say that one stage *enables* another if the second stage can complete only after the first stage is complete. We say that a stage enables another stage *repeatedly* if the second stage can be executed more than once after the first stage is complete. We say that a repeated execution of a stage enables another if the second stage can be executed only after the other stage is executed more than once.

We note that, if one stage enables another, it is not necessary that all of the enabled stage occur after the enabling stage. We only require that the enabled stage not be able to complete until the enabling stage has completed.

The motivation for the division of an attack into stages, one of which can enable another, possibly repeatedly, is that, even if the first stage of an attack is relatively difficult, if it enables repeatedly a second stage which is relatively easy to execute, an intruder is more likely to find it worthwhile to bear the expense of the first stage.

We also have the notion of the scope of a stage. This is the window during which a stage can be completed. For example, if a session key is compromised during a protocol, it can be used by the intruder to impersonate an honest participant, until the session ends. Thus the scope of the impersonation stage is in this case limited by the life of the session. If the protocol is well designed, the intruder cannot use the compromised key to initiate a new session.

### Components of Attack Stages for Cryptographic Protocols

Now that we have given the preliminary conditions, we turn to our example problem, cryptographic protocols, and describe some of the components that might make up a stage of an attack.

Cryptographic protocols are protocols that use cryptography to ensure that parties can cooperate when communicating across a hostile network. Thus these protocols must be robust against a communication medium controlled by an intruder who can read all traffic, alter traffic, and may also be a legitimate participant (or a number of legitimate participants) in the system. Based on these assumptions, there are a number of atomic actions that an intruder could perform or take advantage of. We list some of these below.

*Legitimate Execution* An attack stage involves legitimate execution if a legitimate execution of a protocol between two honest parties must have occurred for the stage to complete.

*Passive Eavesdropping* An attack stage involves passive eavesdropping if it makes use of information that the intruder gains from observing message traffic in one or more executions of a protocol.

*Message Insertion* An attack stage involves message insertion if an intruder must generate and send messages in order for the attack to succeed.

*Message Deletion* An attack stage invovles message deletion if an intruder must prevent messages from reaching their destination in order for the attack to succeed.

*Message Modification* An attack stage involves message modification if a message must not only be prevented from reaching its destination, but replaced by another message, in order for the attack to succeed.

*Message Redirection* An attack stage involves message redirection if a message must not only be prevented from reaching its destination, but redirected to a principal other than the intended recipient, in order for the attack to succeed.

*Extra-Protocol Compromise* An attack stage involves extra-protocol compromise if information (such as a key) must be compromised by means not enabled by the protocol in order for the attack to succeed. Examples of extra-protocol compromise would include theft, and cryptanalysis not enabled by earlier stages of the attack.

*Impersonation and Multiple Impersonation* An attack stage involves impersonation if an intruder must impersonate one principal to another in order for the attack to succeed. A stage involves multiple impersonation if an intruder must impersonate more than one principal, or must impersonate a principal to more than one principal.

*Concurrent Execution* An attack stage involves concurrent execution if two or more executions of the protocol, or executions of different protocols, must proceed concurrently in order for the attack to succeed. This class of attacks is the same the class denoted by the term "interleaving attacks" by Syverson in [**Syv94**].

*Cryptanalysis* An attack stage involves cryptanalysis if cryptanalysis must be performed in order for that stage of the attack to succeed. This differs from extra-protocol compromise, in which information can be compromised in a number of ways.

*Use of System Operations* We say an attack stage makes use of system operations if it makes use of cryptographic operations that are available to a legitimate participant in the protocol. In some cases, in which a protocol uses a widely available cryptosystem, the requirement that an attack use system operations may be trivial. In others, such as Meadows' attack [**Mea92**] on the Simmons Selective Broadcast Protocol [**Sim85**], which requires access to a specialized tamper-proof crypto box, access to system operations may require legitimate access to the system on the part of the intruder, or theft of equipment belonging to the system.

*Type Confusion* We say an attack stage makes use of type confusion if it makes use of causing a party to confuse two words or messages of different types, for example, a timestamp with a key.

Many of the attacks that have been discovered against cryptographic protocols, such as [**DS81, Sim85, Mea96, BAN90, DvOW92, AN94**] make use of some combination of these atomic actions. Indeed, there are a number of specialized tools and techniques that reason about a protocol's security against attacks based on these atomic actions [**BAN90, KMM94**]. Thus, we would expect the collection of known attacks based on combinations of these actions to provide a rich source of study for our proposed methodology. In the next section, we present some example of these and show how they would be represented in our system.

## Examples of Applications of the Representation Technique

**Graphical Representation of Attacks.** Our division of attacks into stages that enable each other has the advantage that it can be easily represented graphically. We give an outline for a graphical representation of an attack below. We represent each stage by a box, where the various components in the stage are the various atomic actions that are involved in each stage. If a stage enables another stage, we represent it by an arrow from the first stage to the second. If it enables another stage repeatedly, we represent it by two arrows fanning out. If it repeated execution of one stage is required to enable the other, we represent it by two arrows fanning in. The scope of each stage can be represented at the bottom of the box. At present, scope is not represented graphically, but is described by text in the bottom of the box.

We also need to get a graphical representation of the difficulty of each stage. There are a number of possible ways of doing this. We could use color or size of the boxes representing the stages, color or size or size or type of font, and so forth. In this paper we will use color, or rather, since this is a monochrome proceedings, different shades of gray. Darker shades of gray are used for more difficult stages of the attack, lighter shades for the easier ones.

**The Denning-Sacco Attack on the Needham-Schroeder Protocol.** For the first example of an application of the taxonomy, consider the Denning-Sacco attack on the Needham-Schroeder protocol described above. It proceeds in four stages. In the first stage, two legitimate parties A and B attempt to establish a session key for communication between each other, and the protocol proceeds at least to the point at which A passes on the key to B. In the second stage, which is enabled by the first, the intruder observes the messages passed in the protocol. This stage involves passive eavesdropping only. In the third stage, the key is compromised. This involves off-line compromise only, since the compromise is not necessarily enabled by the second stage. In the final stage, which is enabled by the second and third stages, the intruder replays a message learned from the second stage to B, pretending that it is sent by A. This stage involves message insertion and impersonation. The intruder then engages in a conversation with B to prove to B that the intruder has knowledge of the key, which requires not only impersonation, but use of the system operations encryption and decryption. Since B's half of the conversation is intended for A, the intruder may also have to prevent B's messages from reaching A. If this is the case, then the stage also involves message destruction.

We note that, if keys are well-protected, then the third stage of the protocol may be difficult. However, the first three stages enable repeatedly a fourth stage which involves impersonation, message insertion, use of system operations, and possibly message destruction. If these operations are considered relatively easy in the context in which the protocol is used, the fact that the fourth stage is enabled repeatedly may make the attack worth attempting in spite of the expense of the second stage. Moreover, the scope of the final stage is limited only be replacing A's master key.

We illustrate the attack in Figure 1. Note that we color the key compromise box dark gray to represent the difficulty of that stage. The final stage is colored light gray to indicate that this stage, while not as difficult as the key compromise stage, is not entirely trivial.

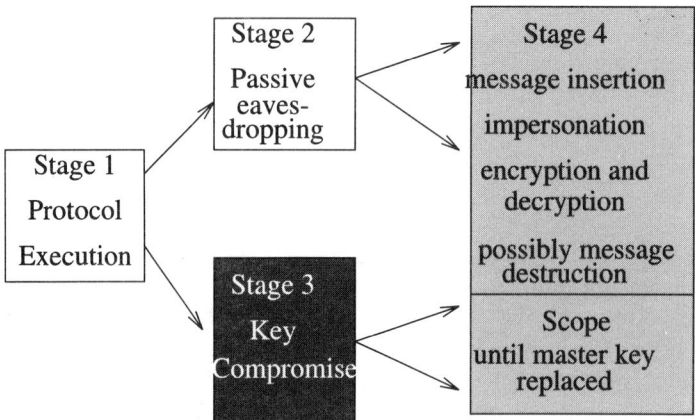

Fig 1. Needham-Schroeder Protocol

**The SSL Protocol.** As a third example, consider the attack found in [**BLS**[+]**95**] on an old draft of the Netscape SSL protocol Version 3.0 [**HE95**]. This protocol allows for clients and server to exchange keys and negotiate which cryptographic algorithms are to be used. Sessions may be reinitiated using the same key. In [**HE95**] the authentication of client to server authenticated only the client's identity and keys being used. It did not authenticate the algorithm being used, or whether or not the session was a new one or a reinitiated one. Thus, if a client was involved in a session using weak cryptography, and an intruder was able to compromise its key, the intruder could initiate a new session with the server using the compromised key, possibly designating a stronger cryptographic algorithm. When the server attempted to authenticate the client in the new session, the intruder could initiate a "man-in-the-middle" attack to cause the client to authenticate itself to the server. Since the authentication data did not contain any information about the algorithm used, the intruder could thus impersonate the client in a session apparently using a strong algorithm. Thus, for example, if the server restricted certain functions to sessions involving high-security algorithms, this attack allowed an intruder to bypass them. [1]

This attack has a number of stages, as follows. In the first stage, the client initiates the protocol using a weak algorithm. This enables the second stage, in which the session key is compromised. The third stage, the man-in-the-middle attack, involves simultaneous impersonation of server to client and client to server, and message redirection. This is enabled repeatedly, but its scope is limited by the completion of the original session. After that, the client will not participate in the man-in-the-middle attack. This is illustrated in Figure 2. Here, we again color the key compromise stage gray, although not as dark as before, since key compromise in real time, although not impossible for weak cryptosystems, is still a challenge. Note that the difficulty of this stage can change if assumptions about the system change. That is, the longer sessions tend to last, the easier this stage gets.

---

[1] In a more recent draft of SSL Version 3.0 [**FKK96**], this problem is avoided by having the client respond by using the signature scheme in its certificate to sign data including a hash of all the previous messages that had been sent in the handshake protocol.

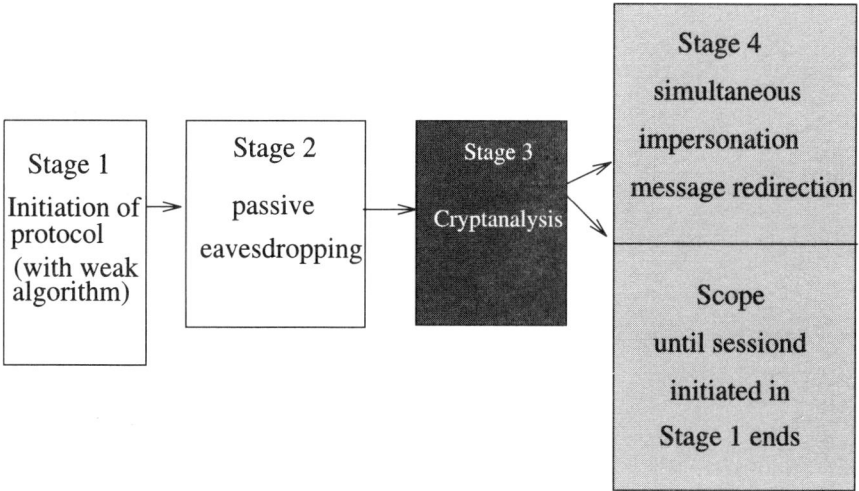

Fig. 2: SSL Protocol

We note that the likelyhood of this attack depends upon a tradeoff between the difficulty of the second stage and the scope of the third stage. If the scope of the third is broad (that is, sessions last for a long time), then the difficulty of compromising the key can be higher. Likewise, if it is easy to compromise the key, the scope of the third stage could be narrower.

## Shostack's Attack on the Security Dynamics Client/Server Protocol

The last example we give is an attack that was first presented at this workshop and is published in these proceedings [Sho]. In the paper, the protocol is described for the case of a UNIX workstation running Security Dynamics' sdshell program. The protocol works by having sdshell communicate with both the user and security server (ACE/server) to obtain the appropriate authentication information. Both sdshell and user share authentication information with the server. The user shares a passcode which is updated by adding one to it at regular intervals. The sdshell shares a conventional cryptographic key with the server.

The protocol works roughly follows. First the user logs into the workstation. Sdshell notifies ACE/server, which responds with a timestamp. Sdshell asks the user for a passcode, which is at the user's discretion. Once sdshell receives the passcode, it calculates an authenticator by taking a hash of its IP address, the timestamp returned by the server, and the passcode. This is divided into four parts. The sdshell encrypts the first part under the key it shares with the server and sends it to the server together with the ID of the user. The server decrypts it, and then calculates the second part of the authenticator from passcode, IP address, and the timestamp it sent. It uses this to encrypt the appropriate authorization, which is sent back to the sdshell.

The problem here, as Shostack noted, is that each part of the authenticator can be guessed or created by an intruder. The hash function is available in the underground literature. IP addresses are easily available. Granularity of timestamps is coarse in this system, so they can also be easily guessed or obtained from the server. Finally, the passcode is verified only by the server, not sdshell, so in order to fool the server, any passcode will do.

The attack proceeds as follows. The attacker finds a port which the sdshell will use to receive traffic from the ACE/server. The attacker telnets to a target machine. It enters a user name and password, which it has found by standard sniffing techniques. It requests and receives a timestamp T from the ACE/Server. It chooses a passcode P and computes a hash of P, T, and the IP address. It also sends P to the sdshell. But, instead of waiting to hear back from the server, it encrypts the authorization it desires with the second part of the hash and send it to the sdshell on the appropriate port.

We represent the attack as follows. We have eight stages. In the first, the attacker finds user name and password. In the third it finds the hash function. In the second it finds out the timestamp. The first stage we color light gray, since it requires some effort on the part of the attacker. We color the second and third stage a very light gray, because some effort may be used to find out the timestamp and the hash function. The first stage enables repeatedly the fourth stage, which is logging in. The second and third stages enable the fifth stage, which is computing the hash function. Again, the third stage enables the fifth stage repeatedly, but the second stage must be enacted anew each time. Stage 4 enables Stage 6, the entering of the passcode, while stage 5 enables Stage 7, the sending of the encrypted access message. Finally, Stages 6 and 7 enables stage 8, the obtaining of the authorization. This is illustrated in Figure 4 below.

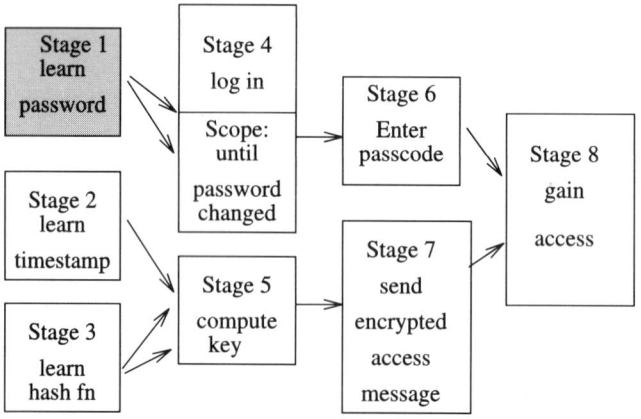

Fig. 3: Attack on Security Dynamics Client/Server Protocol

## Conclusion

In this paper we described a way of representing attacks in terms of the stages of the attack, the relationship between them, and the scope of the stages. We have shown how this representation can be applied to an example application area: evaluation of attacks on cryptographic protocols. However, the our approach should apply to other types of attacks as well.

Our planned use for this representation method is to use it to evaluate risk for a system. Our hope is that the representation of attacks in a simple, graphical manner, that describes first, what must be done to produce each stage and secondly, what payoff is provided by each stage in terms of scope and repeatability will make it easier to compare the threat posed by different attacks and thus to make the appropriate choices.

We note that there are a number of ways of extending this approach. For example, there are some concepts that we need better graphical representations for. Our representation of scope does not make much use of graphics, but relies upon text. It would be useful if we could find a more graphical way of representing this. Also, our it would be helpful to have a way of representing the other relationships between stages besides enabling. For example, in some attacks it may be necessary for two stages to execute simultaneously. It would be helpful to have a way to represent relations like these. It would also be helpful if we had a way to tie our representation of our the difficulty of attacks to our assumptions about the system; this would probably require automated support. Finally, we note that the atomic acts that are represented here, such as key compromise, impersonation, and so forth, are themselves often complex activities, which themselves could be represented using our method. Thus one possible way of extending this method to a hierarchical approach in which actions that are atomic at one level of abstraction are complex at another. This should give us a cleaner way of representing complex activities, and is something that we plan to investigate in the future.

## References

[AN94] Martín Abadi and Roger Needham, *Prudent engineering practice for cryptographic protocols*, 1994 IEEE Computer Society Symposium on Research in Security and Privacy, IEEE Computer Society Press, May 1994, pp. 122–136.

[BAN90] Michael Burrows, Martín Abadi, and Roger Needham, *A logic of authentication*, ACM Transactions in Computer Systems **8** (1990), no. 1, 18–36.

[BCK90] Deborah Boudeau, Frederick Chase, and Sharon Kass, *ANSSR: A tool for risk analysis of networked systems*, Proceedings of the 13th National Computer Security Conference, NSA/NIST, October 1-4 1990, pp. 687–696.

[BLS+95] Josh Benaloh, Butler Lampson, Daniel Simon, Terence Spies, and Bennett Yee, *Private communication technology protocol*, Internet Draft PCT-01, Microsoft Corporation, September 1995.

[Dac94] M. Dacier, *Towards quantitative evaluation of computer security*, Ph.D. thesis, Institut National Polytechnique de Toulouse, December 1994.

[DD94] M. Dacier and Y. Deswarte, *The privilege graph: An extension of the typed access matrix model*, Proceedings of ESORICS '94, Springer-Verlag, November 1994, pp. 319–334.

[DDK96] M. Dacier, Y. Deswarte, and M. Kaaniche, *Models and tools for quantitative assessment of operation security*, 12th International Information Security Conference (S. K. Katsikas and D. Gritzalis, eds.), Chapman and Hall, May 1996, pp. 177–186.

[DS81] D. E. Denning and G. M. Sacco, *Timestamps in key distribution protocols*, Communications of the ACM **24** (1981), no. 8, 198–208.

[DvOW92] Whitfield Diffie, Paul C. van Oorschot, and Michael J. Wiener, *Authentication and authenticated key exchanges*, Designs, Codes, and Cryptography **2** (1992), 107–125.

[FKK96] Alan O. Freier, Philip Karlton, and Paul C. Kocher, *The SSL protocol, version 3.0*, Internet Draft, available at ftp://ietf.cnri.reston.va.us/internet-drafts/draft-freier-ssl-version3-01.txt, March 1996.

[HE95] K. Hickman and T. Elgamal, *The SSL protocol, version 3*, Internet Draft, June 1995.

[KMM94] Richard Kemmerer, Catherine Meadows, and Jonathan Millen, *Three systems for cryptographic protocol analysis*, Journal of Cryptology **7** (1994), no. 2.

[LBF+93]  Bev Littlewood, Sarah Brocklehurst, Norman Felton, Peter Mellor, Stella Page, David Wright, John Dobson, John McDermid, and Dieter Gollmann, *Towards operational measures of computer security*, Journal of Computer Security **2** (1993), no. 2-3, 211–229.
[Mea92]  C. Meadows, *Applying formal methods to the analysis of a key management protocol*, Journal of Computer Security **1** (1992), 5–53.
[Mea96]  Catherine Meadows, *The NRL Protocol Analyzer: An overview*, Journal of Logic Programming **26** (1996), no. 2, 113–131.
[NS78]  R. M. Needham and M. D. Schroeder, *Using encryption for authentication in large networks of computers*, Communications of the ACM **21** (1978), no. 12, 993–999.
[ODK97]  Rodolphe Ortalo, Yves Deswarte, and Mohamed Kaaniche, *Experimenting with quantitative evaluation tools for monitoring operational security*, Proceedings of the Sixth Working Conference on Dependable Computing for Critical Applications, IEEE Computer Society Press, 1997, To appear.
[Sho97]  Adam Shostack, *Apparent weaknesses in the Security Dynamics client/server protocol*, Proceedings of the DIMACS Workshop on Network Threats, AMS, 1997.
[Sim85]  G. J. Simmons, *How to (selectively) broadcast a secret*, Proceedings of the 1985 Symposium on Security and Privac, IEEE Computer Society Press, April 1985, pp. 108–113.
[Syv94]  Paul Syverson, *A taxonomy of replay attacks*, Proceedings of the Computer Security Foundations Workshop VII, IEEE Computer Society Press, June 1994.

NAVAL RESEARCH LABORATORY, CENTER FOR HIGH ASSURANCE COMPUTER SYSTEMS, CODE 5543, WASHINGTON, DC 20375

*E-mail address*: `meadows@itd.nrl.navy.mil`

# Verifying Privacy Enhanced Mail Functions with Higher Order Logic

## Dan Zhou and Shiu-Kai Chin

ABSTRACT. Security properties such as privacy, authentication, and integrity are of increasing importance to networked systems([**KAU**]). Systems with security requirements typically must operate with a high degree of confidence. We show how the message structures of Privacy Enhanced Mail (PEM, [**LIN, BAL**]) and the functions on PEM structures have the desired implementation-independent security properties. Higher-order logic ([**AND**]) and the HOL theorem-prover([**GOR**]) are used to precisely relate security properties to system specifications. The structures of MIC-CLEAR and ENCRYPTED messages are modeled as tuples of fields. Each of these fields is modeled as a type which takes only a limited set of values as valid ([**MEL**]). Security functions for checking privacy, integrity, source authentication and non-repudiation of received messages are defined in HOL. They take as parameters a subset of fields defined above. It is proved that mail messages have these security properties if-and-only-if mail messages satisfy the security functions.

## 1. Introduction

The increasing use of local and wide area networks has increased interest in secure communication where the underlying network itself is insecure. Techniques using encryption, source authentication, message hashing, and digital signatures are used to provide secure communications over insecure networks.

When building secure networked communications systems a fundamental question is, *"how will we precisely understand the security requirements and by what means will we assure that our designs satisfy the requirements?"*

The engineering view we adopt is to use techniques which answer: 1) What objects are in our design? 2) What are the operations on the objects? and 3) How is it known if the objects have the desired properties? For secure electronic mail, the objects of interest are electronic mail messages. Messages have defined structures. Security functions and services are determined by the particular message type or structure. Defining message structures as types aids in proving that implementation-specific functions and services satisfy system-wide security requirements which are implementation independent.

---

1991 *Mathematics Subject Classification.* Primary 68-06.

This research was supported in part by Rome Laboratory and the Air Force Office of Scientific Research.

To illustrate this, we focus on Privacy Enhanced Mail (PEM) [**LIN**] as an example. The techniques we use on PEM are applicable to other message formats and systems, e.g. the National Security Agency's MISSI (Multilevel Information System Security Initiative) system, [**NSA**].

The rest of the paper is organized as follows. An overview of PEM is given in Section 2. Section 3 illustrates how security functions are described in the Higher Order Logic theorem prover, HOL, [**GOR**]. Section 4 briefly describes how message structure is defined in HOL. Section 5 describes message-specific security functions and correctness properties in HOL. We conclude in Section 6.

## 2. Privacy Enhanced Mail

**2.1. Overview.** PEM adds encryption, source authentication, integrity protection and non-repudiation to plain text email. PEM is documented in four *Request for Comments* (RFC) documents. RFC 1421 [**LIN**] describes message encryption, authentication procedures and formats. RFC 1422 describes certificate-based key management. RFC 1423 [**BAL**] describes algorithms. RFC 1424 describes key certification.

PEM as defined by RFC 1421 supports the following security properties: 1) **privacy** – the ability to keep anyone but the intended recipient from reading the message; 2) **authentication** – reassurance to the recipient of the identity of the sender; 3) **integrity** – reassurance to the recipient that the message has not been altered since it was transmitted by the sender; and 4) **non-repudiation** – reassurance to the recipient that he can prove to a third party that the originator did send the message.

**2.2. PEM Message Structure.** There are five types of PEM messages: 1) *ENCRYPTED*, 2) *MIC-CLEAR*, 3) *MIC-ONLY*, 4) *CRL*, and 5) *CRL-RETRIEVAL-REQUEST*. ENCRYPTED, MIC-CLEAR, and MIC-ONLY messages have secret key and public key variants. In this paper, only the public key variant is considered.

By examining each field in a message, we obtain 1) the message text itself which may or may not be encoded or encrypted, and 2) the necessary information to determine its security properties, i.e. authenticity, integrity, non-repudiation and means of encryption. Message structure and contents imply the message type and security services that must be applied.

**2.3. Security Functions.** Privacy is achieved by encryption. Authentication is achieved using secrets. Integrity is obtained by digital signatures, which are the signed message digests. Non-repudiation is checked by signed message.

2.3.1. *Encryption.* There are two types of encryption: secret or *symmetric* key cryptography and public or *asymmetric* key cryptography. Symmetric key cryptography uses the same key for both encryption and decryption. In public or asymmetric key cryptography, different keys are used for encryption and decryption.

2.3.2. *Authentication.* Encryption is used for authenticating or verifying identities. The idea behind authentication is for the person or system to prove it has knowledge of a private key to validate its identity.

For the authentication procedures to work, cryptographic information for users must be available and *certified* by some authority. Authentication in PEM is done using *certificates*. Certificates are data structures which contain the public information of users.

2.3.3. *Hash Functions*. Hash functions take a message of arbitrary length and return a fixed-length string. Hashes are also known as *message digests* or *one-way transformations*. Hash functions have the following properties:

- If $h(m_0)$ denotes the hash of a message $m_0$, there is no substantially easier way to find an $m$ whose hash is $h(m_0)$ without going through all values of $m$ to search for $h(m_0)$.
- It is computationally infeasible to find two values of $m$ which hash to the same value.

Ideally hash functions are "one-to-one" functions, i.e.

$$\forall m_1\ m_2.\ (h(m_1) = h(m_2)) \supset m_1 = m_2$$

Hashes are used for integrity checking. A signed hash of a message is sent with the message as the message integrity code (MIC). The recipient checks the integrity of the received message by computing the hash or message digest of the received message and verifying the received signed message digest against the computed hash.

## 3. Security Functions and Properties in HOL

A person is identified by his/her keys. In public key cryptography, the person is identified by a public key which is known to everyone. Since a private key belongs to only one owner, the corresponding public key uniquely identifies that person. In secret key cryptography, two or more people who share a secret key are identified by that secret; a key uniquely identifies the group that shares it.

**3.1. Retrieval.** In PEM ENCRYPTED messages, two types of encryption keys are used. 1) Data Encryption Keys (DEKs) are used for encrypting message text and for message integrity codes (MICs). DEKs are randomly generated by a sender and sent to a receiver as a part of the PEM message. 2) Interchange Keys (IKs) are used to encrypt DEKs for transmission within messages. IKs are a receiver's public keys.

To retrieve a plaintext message, the recipient retrieves the DEK first using his/her private key, then retrieves the plaintext message using DEK. The following theorem shows that the DEK is retrievable when 1) DEK is encrypted using the intended recipient's public key, and the encrypted DEK is decrypted using the recipient's private key; 2) *decryptP* is the inverse of *encryptP*; 3) the received ciphertext is the transmitted ciphertext; and 4) the recipient of the message is the intended recipient. A similar theorem for message retrieval is also shown.

THEOREM 3.1. *DEK_retrievable*

$\vdash \forall encryptP\ decryptP\ MESSAGE0\ txmsg\ ekeyIR\ dkeyIR\ rxmessage\ rxmsg\ dkeyR.$
  $(txmsg = encryptP\ MESSAGE0\ ekeyIR) \supset$
  $(rxmessage = decryptP\ rxmsg\ dkeyR) \supset$
  $(\forall m.\ decryptP\ (encryptP\ m\ ekeyIR)\ dkeyIR = m) \supset (rxmsg = txmsg) \supset$
  $(dkeyR = dkeyIR) \supset (rxmessage = MESSAGE0)$

TABLE 1. Parameters used in Security Functions

| | |
|---|---|
| $DEK$ | Data Encryption Key |
| $MESSAGE0, message$ | the original plaintext |
| $dKEY0, ekey$ | originator's public & private key |
| $dkey$ | private key |
| $dkeyIR, ekeyIR$ | intended recipient's private & public key |
| $dkeyR$ | recipient's private key |
| $encryptP, decryptP$ | public key encryption & decryption function |
| $encryptS, decryptS$ | secret key encryption & decryption function |
| $hash$ | message digest algorithm |
| $mic$ | digital signature of the plaintext |
| $rxkey$ | received secret key |
| $sign, verify$ | public key signature generation & verification function |
| $signature$ | signed plaintext |
| $txiv, rxiv$ | transmitted & received initial vector |
| $txmessage, rxmessage$ | transmitted and received plaintext |
| $txmic, rxmic$ | transmitted & received digital signature of the plaintext |
| $txmsg, rxmsg$ | transmitted and received ciphertext |

THEOREM 3.2. $message\_retrievable$

$\vdash \forall encryptS\ decryptS\ MESSAGE0\ txmsg\ DEK\ txiv\ rxmessage\ rxmsg\ rxkey\ rxiv.$

$\quad (txmsg = encryptS\ MESSAGE0\ DEK\ txiv) \supset$

$\quad (rxmessage = decryptS\ rxmsg\ rxkey\ rxiv) \supset$

$\quad (\forall m.\ decryptS\ (encryptS\ m\ DEK\ txiv)\ DEK\ txiv = m) \supset (rxmsg = txmsg) \supset$

$\quad (rxiv = txiv) \supset (rxkey = DEK) \supset (rxmessage = MESSAGE0)$

**3.2. Privacy.** The following theorem shows that the original plaintext message is confidential, when 1) the message is properly encrypted using DEK; 2) anything encrypted by a secret key can only be retrieved by the same key; and 3) communication channels are ideal. The confidentiality of DEK can be shown in a similar way.

THEOREM 3.3. $message\_confidential$

$\vdash \forall encryptS\ decryptS\ MESSAGE0\ txmsg\ DEK\ txiv\ rxmessage\ rxmsg\ rxkey\ rxiv.$

$\quad (txmsg = encryptS\ MESSAGE0\ DEK\ txiv) \supset$

$\quad (rxmessage = decryptS\ rxmsg\ rxkey\ rxiv) \supset$

$\quad (\forall m.decryptS\ (encryptS\ m\ DEK\ txiv)\ DEK\ txiv = m) \supset$

$\quad (\forall m\ k1\ k2.\ (decryptS\ (encryptS\ m\ k1\ txiv)\ k2\ txiv = m) \supset (k1 = k2)) \supset$

$\quad (rxmsg = txmsg) \supset (rxiv = txiv) \supset$

$\quad (rxmessage = MESSAGE0) \supset (rxkey = DEK)$

**3.3. Integrity.** $is\_Intact$ is defined for message integrity checking. It declares that both the message and its digital signature are intact if the verification of the digital signature of the original message against the hash of the retrieved message succeeds. See Table 1 for the parameters used in the definition.

## VERIFYING PRIVACY ENHANCED MAIL FUNCTIONS

DEFINITION 3.4. *is_Intact*

$\vdash_{def} \forall verify\ hash\ message\ mic\ ekey.$
$is\_Intact\ verify\ hash\ message\ mic\ ekey =$
$verify\ (hash\ message)\ mic\ ekey$

*is_Intact* is true if-and-only-if the received message is identical to the one transmitted. The correctness theorem is proved using the definition of *is_Intact* with the following assumptions: 1) Hash function is one-to-one; 2) MIC field is the signed message digest; 3) Signature of a specific message can be verified through the signer's public key.

THEOREM 3.5. *is_Intact_msg_Correct*

$\vdash \forall verify\ sign\ hash\ txmessage\ rxmessage\ txmic\ rxmic\ ekey\ dkey.$
$(txmic = sign\ (hash\ txmessage)\ dkey) \supset (rxmic = txmic) \supset$
$(\forall m_1\ m_2.\ (hash\ m_1 = hash\ m_2) \supset (m_1 = m_2)) \supset$
$(\forall s_1\ s_2.\ verify\ s_1\ (sign\ s_2\ dkey)\ ekey = s_1 = s_2) \supset$
$((rxmessage = txmessage)$
$= is\_Intact\ verify\ hash\ rxmessage\ rxmic\ ekey)$

When the received MIC is not the same as the one sent by the originator, the following theorem proves that the recipient cannot be sure of the integrity of either the MIC or plaintext message.

THEOREM 3.6. *not_Intact*

$\vdash \forall verify\ sign\ hash\ MESSAGE0\ txmic\ rxmic\ ekey\ dKEY0.$
$(txmic = sign\ (hash\ MESSAGE0)\ dKEY0) \supset$
$(\forall m_1\ m_2.\ verify\ m_1\ m_2\ ekey = (m_2 = sign\ m_1\ dKEY0)) \supset$
$(\forall m_1\ m_2\ dkey_1\ dkey_2.\ (sign\ m_1\ dkey_1 = sign\ m_2\ dkey_2)$
$\supset (m_1 = m_2) \wedge (dkey_1 = dkey_2)) \supset$
$\neg(rxmic = txmic) \supset \neg(is\_Intact\ verify\ hash\ MESSAGE0\ rxmic\ ekey)$

**3.4. Source Authentication.** The function *is_Authentic* checks the source authenticity of a received message. If verification of the retrieved signature against the retrieved message succeeds, the recipient can be sure of the source of the received message. See Table 1 for parameters used in the definition.

DEFINITION 3.7. *is_Authentic*

$\vdash_{def} \forall verify\ hash\ message\ mic\ ekey.$
$is\_Authentic\ verify\ hash\ message\ mic\ ekey =$
$verify\ (hash\ message)\ mic\ ekey$

The source authentication check *is_Authentic* is true if and only if the originator of the message is the one identified by the public key we use to verify the signature. The correctness of the check can be proved if: 1) Hash function is one-to-one; 2) MIC field is the signed message hash; and 3) It is computationally infeasible to find two messages and two private keys which can generate same signature.

THEOREM 3.8. *is_Authentic_msg_correct*.

⊢ ∀*verify sign hash message* $MESSAGE0$ *txmic rxmic ekey* $dKEY0$ *dkey*.

($rxmic = txmic$) ⊃ ($txmic = sign(hashMESSAGE0)dkey$) ⊃

(∀$m_1$ $m_2$. ($hash$ $m_1 = hash$ $m_2$) = $m_1 = m_2$) ⊃

(∀$m_1$ $m_2$ $dkey_2$. *verify* $m_1(sign$ $m_2$ $dkey_2)ekey$

= ($m_1 = m_2$) ∧ ($dkey_2 = dKEY0$)) ⊃

(($dkey = dKEY0$) ∧ ($message = MESSAGE0$) =

*is_Authentic verify hash message rxmic ekey*)

If the first assumption is not satisfied, the source authentication fails and the recipient of the message cannot be sure of the source of the message. The correctness of this statement can be shown in a similar theorem to *not_Intact*.

If hash function is not one-to-one, we can define an equivalence relation ($\eta$ $hash$) on the message space:

∀$m_1$ $m_2$. ($\eta$ $hash$) $m_1$ $m_2$ = ($hash$ $m_1 = hash$ $m_2$)

Function *is_Authentic* will either succeed or fail for all the messages in an equivalence class induced by ($\eta$ $hash$). Instead of identifying the source of a single message $MESSAGE0$ as $dKEY0$, *is_Authentic* will take $dKEY0$ as the originator for every message in equivalence class

$Ec$ ($MESSAGE0$) = ∀$m$. ($\eta$ $hash$) $m$ $MESSAGE0$

This is the problem raised in [**MIT**].

**3.5. Non-Repudiation.** Function *is_non_Deniable* is the security check of non-repudiation property of the message system. It checks the non-deniability of the sender of the message by verifying the signature against the received plaintext. See Table 1 for parameters used in the definition.

DEFINITION 3.9. *is_non_Deniable*

⊢$_{def}$ ∀*verify message signature ekey*.

*is_non_Deniable verify message signature ekey* =

*verify message signature ekey*

The non-repudiation check defined above is true if and only if the received message is generated by the originator whose public key is *ekey*, and the originator cannot deny having sent the message. This claim is true under these assumptions: 1) Hash function is one-to-one; 2) MIC field is the signed message digest; 3) It is computationally infeasible to find two message and two private keys which can generate same signature. Its corresponding correctness theorem is proved using the definition of *is_non_Deniable*.

THEOREM 3.10. *is_non_Deniable_msg*

⊢ ∀*verify sign hash message* $MESSAGE0$ *txmic rxmic ekey* $dKEY0$ *dkey*.

($rxmic = txmic$) ⊃ ($txmic = sign(hashMESSAGE0)dkey$) ⊃

(∀$m_1$ $m_2$. ($hash$ $m_1 = hash$ $m_2$) = $m_1 = m_2$) ⊃

(∀$m_1$ $m_2$ $dkey_2$. *verify* $m_1(sign$ $m_2$ $dkey_2)ekey$

= ($m_1 = m_2$) ∧ ($dkey_2 = dKEY0$)) ⊃

(($dkey = dKEY0$) ∧ ($message = MESSAGE0$) =

*is_non_Deniable verify* (*hash message*) *rxmic ekey*)

When the received MIC is not the same as the transmitted MIC, the recipient cannot show to a third party that the originator has indeed sent the message. The correctness of this statement can be shown in a similar theorem to *not_Intact*.

In this paper, all assumptions for correctness theorem are antecedents of nested implications. There are no assumed axioms.

The definitions and properties developed in this section are independent of any particular implementation. What we must do is to link the particular implementation to the general definitions and properties. For this we must define the structure of PEM messages.

## 4. Message Structure in HOL

PEM messages are modeled as *8-tuples*. However, not all *8-tuples* are valid PEM messages. When a proper subset of possible representations is identified as a *new type*, reasoning about messages is simplified because only valid representations are considered. The next section briefly illustrates the concepts of defining new types in HOL.

### 4.1. Type Definition in HOL.
New types are introduced in HOL by identifying a subset of an existing type whose properties correspond to the properties of the new type, [**MEL**]. *Isomorphic* (one-to-one and onto) mappings between elements of the new type and elements of the subset of the existing type are defined. One mapping is the *representation* of the new type in terms of the existing type. The other is the *abstraction* of the existing type into the new type.

A valid representation function is *any* function which is an isomorphism. Objects having a property $P$ are denoted by Hilbert's $\varepsilon$-operator, [**MEL**]. The semantics of $\varepsilon$ are given below.

$$\vdash \forall P.\ (\exists x.\ P\ x) \supset P(\varepsilon x.\ P\ x)$$

When defining a new type from an existing one, $P$ identifies the subset of the existing type used to represent the new type. $TYPE\_DEF$ defines the properties of a valid representation.

$$\vdash_{def} TYPE\_DEF\ P\ rep = (\forall a_1\ a_2.\ rep\ a_1 = rep\ a_2 \supset a_1 = a_2) \wedge$$
$$(\forall r.\ P\ r = \exists a.\ r = rep\ a)$$

$REP = \varepsilon\ rep.\ TYPE\_DEF\ P\ rep$ is any valid representation, $ABS\ r = \varepsilon\ a.\ (r = REP\ a)$ defines a valid abstraction function based on $REP$.

### 4.2. MIC_info as a Type.
We focus on the *MIC_info* portion of a message. *MIC_info* is modeled as a *3-tuple* where the first element identifies the hash function used to compute the MIC; the second element is the signature algorithm used to encrypt the MIC; and the third element is the signed message digest for the transmitted message.

Valid *MIC_Info* fields are a *proper* subset of all *3-tuples* of ($algid \times algid \times asymsignmic$). The predicate $is\_MIC\_info$ identifies the valid *3-tuples* for *MIC_Info*. The representation function $REP\_MIC\_info$ and the abstraction function $MIC\_info$ are defined following the type definition procedure in HOL.

Now various accessor functions can be defined to get the hash algorithm, signature algorithm, and signed message digest portions of the *MIC_Info* field.

As the algorithm names in the *MIC_info* field are just names and not the actual hash and signature functions, we define signature and hash selector functions which take a function name and return its corresponding function.

## 5. Security Functions for PEM Messages

With the definition of selector and accessor functions defined above, we can define security functions for specific PEM message format. As an example, we will show the *integrity* checking function for MIC-CLEAR messages and the *source authentication* checking function for ENCRYPTED messages.

### 5.1. Function for MIC-CLEAR Messages.
MIC-CLEAR messages are modeled as *8-tuples*: (*preeb* × *proctype* × *contentdomain* × *origid_asymm* × *issuer-certificate* × *MIC_info* × *pemtext* × *posteb*).

The integrity checking function $MIC\_CLEAR\_is\_Intact$ for MIC-CLEAR messages is defined as the general integrity function *is_Intact*, with its parameters specialized with the hash and signature selection functions.

DEFINITION 5.1. $MIC\_CLEAR\_is\_Intact$

    $MIC\_CLEAR\_is\_Intact$ msg =
        let micInfo = get_MIC_CLEAR_MIC_Info msg in
        let ekey =
            get_Key_from_ID (get_OriginatorAsymID_info msg) in
        is_Intact (MIC_sign_select micInfo)
            (MIC_hash_select micInfo) (get_MIC_CLEAR_text msg)
            (get_MIC_mic micInfo) ekey

Given the definition of $MIC\_CLEAR\_is\_Intact$ and the general correctness theorem *is_Intact*, we can prove the following correctness theorem for $MIC\_CLEAR\_is\_Intact$. It states that under similar assumptions to the general *is_Intact* correctness theorem, $MIC\_CLEAR\_is\_Intact$ is true if-and-only-if the transmitted and received messages are the same.

THEOREM 5.2.

    ⊢ ∀mic_clear_msg sign txmessage dkey.
        let micInfo = get_MIC_CLEAR_MIC_Info mic_clear_msg in
        let ekey = get_Key_from_ID
            (get_Originator_AsymID_info mic_clear_msg)in
        let hash = MIC_hash_select micInfo and
        verify = MIC_sign_select micInfo and
        rxmessage = get_MIC_CLEAR_text mic_clear_msg in
        (get_MIC_mic micInfo = sign (hash txmessage) dkey) ⊃
        ($\forall m_1\ m_2$. (hash $m_1$ = hash $m_2$) ⊃ ($m_1 = m_2$)) ⊃
        ($\forall m_1\ m_2$. verify $m_1$ (sign $m_2$ dkey) ekey = $m_1 = m_2$) ⊃
        ((txmessage = rxmessage) =
            $MIC\_CLEAR\_is\_Intact$ mic_clear_msg)

## 5.2. Function for ENCRYPTED Messages.

For simplicity, *ENCRYPTED* messages are modeled as *8-tuples*: $(preeb \times proctype \times contentdomain \times dekinfo \times id\_asymmetric \times (certificate)list \times MIC\_info \times (id\_asymmetric \times Key\_info)list \times pemtext \times posteb)$.

The source authentication check function $ENCRYPTED\_is\_Authentic$ is defined as the general source authentication function $is\_Authentic$, with its parameters specialized with the hash and signature selection functions.

DEFINITION 5.3. $ENCRYPTED\_is\_Authentic$
⊢ ∀msg. $ENCRYPTED\_is\_Authentic$ msg =
  let micInfo = getEN_MIC_info msg in
  let ekey = get_Key_from_ID
    (getEN_OriginatorAsymID_info msg) in
  is_Authentic (MIC_sign_select micInfo)
    (MIC_hash_select micInfo) (getEN_msg_message msg)
    (getEN_msg_MIC msg) ekey

Given the definition of $ENCRYPTED\_is\_Authentic$ and the general correctness theorem $is\_Authentic\_msg$, correctness theorem for $ENCRYPTED\_is\_Authentic\_msg$ is proved. It states that under similar assumptions to the general $is\_Authentic\_msg$ correctness theorem, $ENCRYPTED\_is\_Authentic\_msg$ is true if-and-only-if the received original plaintext is sent by the originator identified by the public key stated in the received message.

THEOREM 5.4. $ENCRYPTED\_is\_Authentic\_msg$
⊢ ∀Encrypted_msg sign MESSAGE0 txmic dKEY0 dkey.
  let micInfo = getEN_MIC_info Encrypted_msg in
  let verify = MIC_sign_select micInfo and
  hash = MIC_hash_select micInfo and
  message = getEN_msg_message Encrypted_msg and
  rxmic = getEN_msg_MIC Encrypted_msg and
  ekey = get_Key_from_ID
    (getEN_OriginatorAsymID_infoEncrypted_msg) in
  (rxmic = txmic) ⊃ (txmic = sign (hash MESSAGE0) dkey) ⊃
  (∀$m_1$ $m_2$. (hash $m_1$ = hash $m_2$) = $m_1$ = $m_2$) ⊃
  (∀$m_1$ $m_2$ $dkey_2$.
    verify $m_1$ (sign $m_2$ $dkey_2$) ekey = ($m_1$ = $m_2$) ∧ $dkey_2$ = dKEY0) ⊃
  ((dkey = dKEY0) ∧ (message = MESSAGE0)
    = $ENCRYPTED\_is\_Authentic$ Encrypted_msg)

## 6. Conclusions

This work focuses on verifying the security properties of Privacy Enhanced Mail (PEM). Security properties such as privacy, source authentication, integrity, and non-repudiation are defined independently of any implementation structure. PEM message structures and operations on those structures are shown to have the desired security properties. Various PEM structures are defined as types. Security interpretations are defined as operations on these types.

Properties of cryptographic algorithms are modeled and used as antecedents of a nested implication. Without guarantee of these properties, the security checks defined in the paper would not add much assurance to the design.

All the definitions and proofs are done using the Higher Order Logic (HOL) theorem-prover. While at times the proofs are intricate, the proofs are well within the capabilities of engineers who have been trained to use HOL.

The work done on PEM shows the feasibility of using formal logic and computer assisted reasoning tools to describe and verify relatively complex systems. The advantages of using these methods is the assurance of correctness of the specifications given to implementers. If the specifications are correctly implemented, then the desired security properties will be achieved.

## References

[AND] P. Andrews, *An introduction to Higher Order Logic: to truth through proof*, Academic Press, New York, 1986.

[BAL] D. Balenson, *Privacy enhancement for internet electronic mail: part III: algorithms, modes, and identifiers*, RFC 1423, TIS, February, 1993, ftp: ds.internic.net.

[CHI] Shiu-Kai Chin, John Faust, Joseph Giordano, *Formal Methods Applied to Secure Network Engineering*, IEEE Int. Conf. on Engineering of Complex Computer Systems, Montreal, Quebec, Canada, October 21-25, 1996

[KAU] Charlie Kaufman, Radia Perlman, Mike Speciner, *Network security private communication in a public world*, Prentice Hall, New Jersey, 1995.

[GOR] M.J.C. Gordon, *A proof generating system for higher-order logic*, in *VLSI specification, verification and synthesis*, G. Birtwistle and P. A. Subramanyam, Kluwer, 1987

[LIN] J. Linn, *Privacy enhancement for internet electronic mail: part I: message encryption and authentication procedures*, DEC, RFC 1421, February, 1993, ftp: ds.internic.net.

[MEL] T. Melham, *Automating recursive type definitions in higher order logic*, in *Current Trends in Hardware Verification and Automated Theorem Proving*, G. Birtwistle and P. Subrahmanyam, Springer-Verlag, 1989, 341–386.

[MIT] C. Mitchell, *Multi-destination secure electronic mail*, The Computer Journal, Vol. 32, No. 1, 1989, pp.13-15.

[NSA] National Security Agency, *Network security managers (NSM) functional requirements specification and concept of operations (CONOP)*.

DEPARTMENT OF ELECTRICAL ENGINEERING AND COMPUTER SCIENCE, SYRACUSE UNIVERSITY, SYRACUSE, NEW YORK 13244

*E-mail address*: `danzhou@cat.syr.edu`

DEPARTMENT OF ELECTRICAL ENGINEERING AND COMPUTER SCIENCE, SYRACUSE UNIVERSITY, SYRACUSE, NEW YORK 13244

*E-mail address*: `chin@cat.syr.edu`

# Cryptanalysis of RSA-type Cryptosystems: A Visit

Marc Joye and Jean-Jacques Quisquater

ABSTRACT. This paper surveys RSA-type implementations based on Lucas sequences and on elliptic curves. The main focus is the way how some known attacks on RSA were extended to LUC, KMOV and Demytko's system. It also gives some directions for the choice of the most appropriate RSA-type system for a given application.

## 1. Introduction

In 1978, Rivest, Shamir and Adleman [63] introduced the so-called RSA cryptosystem. Its security mainly relies on the difficulty of factoring carefully chosen large integers.

After this breakthrough, other structures were proposed to produce analogues to RSA. So, Müller and Nöbauer [54, 55] presented a cryptosystem using Dickson polynomials. This system was afterwards slightly modified and rephrased in terms of Lucas sequences by Smith and Lennon [70, 72]. More recently, Koyama, Maurer, Okamoto and Vanstone [41] exhibited new one-way trapdoor functions similar to RSA on elliptic curves, the so-called KMOV cryptosystem. Later, Demytko [20] also pointed out a new one-way trapdoor function on elliptic curves to produce an analogue of RSA.

There are numerous mathematical attacks on RSA. They can basically be classified into three categories independently of the protocol in use for encryption or signature:

1. attacks exploiting the polynomial structure of RSA [11, 14, 25, 29, 47, 57];
2. attacks based on its homomorphic nature [2, 7, 15, 17, 19, 22, 21, 16, 26];
3. attacks resulting of a bad choice of parameters [74].

Most of known attacks on RSA can more or less successfully be extended to their Lucas and elliptic curves based analogues. Rather than reviewing in details all the attacks, we have chosen three representative attacks (one per category) and explain how there were extended. This enables the reader to evaluate the potential danger of a future attack on a RSA-type cryptosystem.

The first category of attacks relies on the polynomial structure of RSA. Since Lucas sequences can be expressed in terms of Dickson polynomials, all these attacks can almost straightforwardly be adapted. Using division polynomials, the same

---

1991 *Mathematics Subject Classification*. Primary 94A60, 11T71; Secondary 11B39, 14H52.

conclusion holds for elliptic curves based cryptosystems. The GCD attack [14] falls into this category.

The second type of attacks does not extend so easily to LUC or Demytko's system, because their non homomorphic nature. Therefore, they apparently seem to be resistant. However, multiplicative attacks can sometimes be rewritten in order to be applicable on these latter systems. We shall illustrate this topic with the common modulus attack [68].

The last category of attacks does not really result from a weakness of RSA but rather from a bad implementation. Parameters have to be carefully chosen. Unfortunately, there is no general recipe to extend this kind of attack. In some cases, attacks remain valid like for the low secret exponents attack [74].

The remaining of this paper is organized as follows. In Section 2, we review the Lucas-based cryptosystems, and the elliptic curves RSA cryptosystems in Section 3. Next, in Section 4, we present the GCD attack, the common modulus failure and the Wiener's attack. We also outline the way they were extended. Finally, we conclude in Section 5.

## 2. Lucas-based cryptosystems

We assume that the reader is familiar with the basic properties of RSA.

### 2.1. Lucas sequences.

DEFINITION 2.1. *Let $P$ and $Q$ be integers, and let $\alpha$ be a root of the polynomial $x^2 - Px + Q$ in the quadratic field $\mathbb{Q}(\sqrt{\Delta})$, where $\Delta = P^2 - 4Q$ is a non-square. Writing $\alpha = \frac{P+\sqrt{\Delta}}{2}$ and its conjugate $\beta = \frac{P-\sqrt{\Delta}}{2}$, the Lucas sequences $\{U_n\}_{n\geq 0}$ and $\{V_n\}_{n\geq 0}$ are given by*

$$U_n(P,Q) = \frac{\alpha^n - \beta^n}{\alpha - \beta} \quad \text{and} \quad V_n(P,Q) = \alpha^n + \beta^n. \tag{2.1}$$

*In particular, $U_0 = 0$, $U_1 = 1$, $V_0 = 2$ and $V_1 = P$.*

PROPOSITION 2.2. *Let $U_i(P,Q)$ and $V_i(P,Q)$, the $i^{\text{th}}$ terms of the Lucas sequences with parameters $P$, $Q$ and $\Delta = P^2 - 4Q$. Then,*

$$V_k^2(P,Q) - \Delta U_k^2(P,Q) = 4Q^k, \tag{2.2}$$
$$U_{mk}(P,Q) = U_k(P,Q)U_m\left(V_k(P,Q), Q^k\right), \tag{2.3}$$
$$V_{mk}(P,Q) = V_m\left(V_k(P,Q), Q^k\right), \tag{2.4}$$
$$2U_{m+k}(P,Q) = U_m(P,Q)V_k(P,Q) + U_k(P,Q)V_m(P,Q), \tag{2.5}$$
$$2V_{m+k}(P,Q) = V_m(P,Q)V_k(P,Q) + \Delta U_m(P,Q)U_k(P,Q). \tag{2.6}$$

□

PROPOSITION 2.3. *Let $\Psi(p) = p - (\Delta/p)$, where $p$ is a prime that does not divide $2\Delta$. Then,*

$$U_{k\Psi(p)+1}(P,1) \equiv U_1(P,1) = 1 \pmod{p}, \tag{2.7}$$
$$V_{k\Psi(p)+1}(P,1) \equiv V_1(P,1) = P \pmod{p}. \tag{2.8}$$

□

Identity (2.8) enables to construct a RSA-like cryptosystem based on Lucas sequences with parameters $P$, $Q = 1$ and $\Delta = P^2 - 4$.

**2.2. LUC [70, 72].** Each user chooses two large primes $p$ and $q$, and publishes the product $n = pq$. Next, he chooses a public encryption key $e$ that is relatively prime to $(p-1)$, $(p+1)$, $(q-1)$ and $(q+1)$. Finally, he computes the secret decryption key $d$ according to

$$(2.9) \qquad ed \equiv 1 \pmod{\Psi(n)},$$

where $\Psi(n) = \ell cm(p - (\Delta/p), q - (\Delta/q))$.

To send a message $m$ to Bob, Alice looks to Bob's public key $e$ and computes the ciphertext $c = V_e(m, 1) \bmod n$. Next, to recover the plaintext $m$, Bob uses his secret decryption key $d$ to obtain

$$(2.10) \qquad m = V_d(c, 1) \bmod n.$$

PROOF. From Equation (2.4) and Proposition 2.3, we have

$$V_d(c, 1) \equiv V_d\bigl(V_e(m, 1), 1\bigr) \equiv V_{de}(m, 1) \equiv m \pmod{n}.$$

□

Apparently, the drawback in this method is that $d$ depends on the message $m$ because $\Delta = m^2 - 4$. In fact, according to the values of $(\Delta/p)$ and $(\Delta/q)$, there are four possibilities for $d$ that satisfy relation (2.9). However, the decryption key corresponding to a given message can be determined *a priori* since

$$\begin{aligned}
\Psi(n) &= \ell cm\bigl(p - (\Delta/p), q - (\Delta/q)\bigr) \\
&= \ell cm\bigl(p - (\Delta U_e^2(m, 1)/p), q - (\Delta U_e^2(m, 1)/q)\bigr) \\
&= \ell cm\left(p - \left(\frac{c^2-4}{p}\right), q - \left(\frac{c^2-4}{q}\right)\right), \text{ by Eq. (2.2)}.
\end{aligned}$$

REMARK 2.4. It is possible to construct a message independent cryptosystem, taking $d$ such that $ed \equiv 1 \pmod{\ell cm(p-1, p+1, q-1, q+1)}$. This method avoids the computation of the two Legendre symbols in the expression of $\Psi(n)$, but it doubles the length of the deciphering key, on average.

## 3. Elliptic curves RSA cryptosystems

### 3.1. Basic facts.

DEFINITION 3.1. Let $K$ be a field of characteristic $\neq 2, 3$, and let $x^3 + ax + b$ (where $a, b \in K$) be a cubic with no multiple roots. An *elliptic curve* $E(a, b)$ over $K$ is the set of points $(x, y) \in K \times K$ satisfying the equation

$$(3.1) \qquad y^2 = x^3 + ax + b$$

together with a single element denoted $\mathcal{O}$ and called the *point at infinity*.

Let $\mathbf{P}, \mathbf{Q} \in E(a, b)$, let $\ell$ be the line connecting $\mathbf{P}$ and $\mathbf{Q}$ (tangent line if $\mathbf{P} = \mathbf{Q}$), and let $\mathbf{T}$ be the third point of intersection of $\ell$ with $E(a, b)$. If $\ell'$ is the line connecting $\mathbf{T}$ and $\mathcal{O}$, then $\mathbf{P} + \mathbf{Q}$ is the point such that $\ell'$ intersects $E(a, b)$ at $\mathbf{T}, \mathcal{O}$ and $\mathbf{P} + \mathbf{Q}$.

PROPOSITION 3.2. *The previous composition law makes $E(a, b)$ into an Abelian group with identity element $\mathcal{O}$.*

□

THEOREM 3.3 (Hasse). *If $K$ is the prime finite field $\mathbb{F}_p$, then the order $m$ of the group $E_p(a,b)$ (i.e. the elliptic curve $E(a,b)$ over $\mathbb{F}_p$) is given by*

(3.2) $$\#E_p(a,b) = p + 1 - a_p,$$

*where $|a_p| \leq 2\sqrt{p}$.* □

DEFINITION 3.4. Let $E_p(a,b)$ be an elliptic curve over the prime field $\mathbb{F}_p$. The *complementary group* of $E_p(a,b)$ is the set of points satisfying relation (3.1) together with $\mathcal{O}$, where $y$ is of the form $u\sqrt{v}$, and $v$ is a fixed non-quadratic residue modulo $p$ and $v \in \mathbb{F}_p$. The complementary group of $E_p(a,b)$ will be denoted $\overline{E_p(a,b)}$.

COROLLARY 3.5. *If $\#E_p(a,b) = 1 + p - a_p$, then $\#\overline{E_p(a,b)} = 1 + p + a_p$.* □

For some special cases, the order and the structure of an elliptic curve can easily be determined.

LEMMA 3.6. *Let $p$ be an odd prime congruent to $2 \bmod 3$. Then the elliptic curve $E_p(0,b)$ is a cyclic group of order $p+1$.* □

LEMMA 3.7. *Let $p$ be a prime congruent to $3 \bmod 4$. If $a$ is a quadratic residue modulo $p$, then $E_p(a,0)$ is a cyclic group of order $p+1$. If $a$ is a non quadratic residue modulo $p$, then $E_p(a,0)$ is a group isomorphic to $\mathbb{Z}_{(p+1)/2} \times \mathbb{Z}_2$ of order $p+1$.* □

**3.2. Elliptic curves over the ring $\mathbb{Z}_n$.** In this paragraph, $n$ will denote the product of two large distinct primes $p$ and $q$.

DEFINITION 3.8. Like the definition over the field $\mathbb{F}_p$, an *elliptic curve* $E_n(a,b)$ over the ring $\mathbb{Z}_n$ is the set of the points $(x,y) \in \mathbb{Z}_n \times \mathbb{Z}_n$ satisfying the equation

(3.3) $$y^2 = x^3 + ax + b \pmod{n}$$

together with the point $\mathcal{O}$.

However, the resulting structure is not a group ; nevertheless a proposition similar to Lagrange's theorem holds.

PROPOSITION 3.9. *Let $E_n(a,b)$ be an elliptic curve over $\mathbb{Z}_n$ such that $\gcd(4a^3 + 27b^2, n) = 1$. If $N_n = \ell\mathrm{cm}(\#E_p(a,b), \#E_q(a,b))$, then*

(3.4) $$\forall \mathbf{P} \in E_n(a,b), \forall k \in \mathbb{Z} : (kN_n + 1)\mathbf{P} = \mathbf{P}.$$

□

It is possible (but very unlikely) that the addition of two points on $E_n(a,b)$ is undefined. In practice, this will cause no problem, because the probability of finding two points such that their sum is undefined is the same than finding the two prime factors of $n$.

Proposition 3.9 seems to establish a RSA-type cryptosystem. However, some problems occur. Suppose that Alice wants to send message $m$ to Bob. Bob fixes an elliptic curve $E_n(a,b)$ over $\mathbb{Z}_n$ and computes $N_n = \ell\mathrm{cm}(\#E_p(a,b), \#E_q(a,b))$. He chooses a public key $e$ that is relatively prime to $N_n$, and computes $d$ such that $ed \equiv 1 \pmod{N_n}$. The values of $e$ and $n$, and the elliptic curve $E_n(a,b)$ are public. To encode the message $m$, Alice represents it, in a publicly known way, as a point $\mathbf{M}$ of the elliptic curve $E_n(a,b)$ (by adding redundancy, for example). Then she computes $\mathbf{C} = e\mathbf{M}$ and sends $\mathbf{C}$ to Bob. To recover the message $m$, Bob uses his secret key $d$ to compute $d\mathbf{C} = de\mathbf{M} = \mathbf{M}$. This scheme is *not* correct because several messages may be represented by the same point $\mathbf{M}$. Therefore, Proposition 3.9 can only be used to construct a signature scheme. Another idea is to let Alice choosing the parameters $a$ and $b$ of the elliptic curve in order to uniquely represent $m$ as a point of the curve. But in that case, $N_n$ (which has to be re-computed by Bob) is not necessarily coprime to $e$. To overcome these drawbacks, new schemes were proposed.

**3.3. KMOV [41].** The KMOV system relies on Lemma 3.6. Each user chooses two primes $p$ and $q$ both congruent to 2 modulo 3, and publishes their product $n = pq$. Next, he selects a public key $e$ relatively prime to $N_n = \ell\text{cm}(p+1, q+1)$ and computes the secret key $d$ such to

(3.5) $$ed \equiv 1 \pmod{N_n}.$$

To send a message $\mathbf{M} = (m_1, m_2)$ to Bob, Alice chooses the parameter $b$ according to

(3.6) $$b = m_2^2 - m_1^3 \bmod n.$$

Next, using Bob's public key $e$, she encrypts $\mathbf{M} \in E_n(0, b)$ as $\mathbf{C} = e\mathbf{M} = (c_1, c_2)$, and sends it to Bob. From $\mathbf{C}$, Bob computes the parameter $b = c_2^2 - c_1^3 \bmod n$. Then, he recovers the original message with its secret key $d$ by computing $\mathbf{M} = d\mathbf{C}$ on the curve $E_n(0, b)$.

REMARK 3.10. As mentioned in [41], from Lemma 3.7, it is also possible to work on a curve of the form $E_n(a, 0)$ by choosing

(3.7) $$a = \frac{m_2^2 - m_1^3}{m_1} \bmod n.$$

**3.4. Demytko [20].** In this cryptosystem, each user chooses once for all the parameters $a$, $b$ and $e$. Let $m$ be the message to be encoded. The Demytko's system is based on the fact that if $m$ (modulo $p$) is not the $x$-coordinate of a point on $E_p(a, b)$, it will be the $x$-coordinate of a point on the twisted curve $\overline{E_p(a, b)}$.

It is useful to introduce some notation. Since the computation of the $y$-coordinate can be avoided (by using the algorithm described in [8], for example), $k \star p_x$ will denote the $x$-coordinate of $k$ times the point $\mathbf{P} = (p_x, p_y)$. To encrypt $m$, Alice computes $c = e \star m$. To decrypt the ciphertext $c$, Bob computes $d_i \star c = d_i e \star m = m$, where the decryption key is chosen according to

(3.8) $$ed_i \equiv 1 \pmod{N_{n,i}} \quad (i = 1, \ldots, 4)$$

with

$$\begin{cases} N_{n,1} = \ell\text{cm}(p+1-a_p, q+1-a_q) & \text{if } (w/p) = 1 \text{ and } (w/q) = 1 \\ N_{n,2} = \ell\text{cm}(p+1-a_p, q+1+a_q) & \text{if } (w/p) = 1 \text{ and } (w/q) \neq 1 \\ N_{n,3} = \ell\text{cm}(p+1+a_p, q+1-a_q) & \text{if } (w/p) \neq 1 \text{ and } (w/q) = 1 \\ N_{n,4} = \ell\text{cm}(p+1+a_p, q+1+a_q) & \text{if } (w/p) \neq 1 \text{ and } (w/q) \neq 1 \end{cases}$$

and $w = c^3 + ac + b \pmod{n}$.

REMARK 3.11. It is possible to construct a message independent cryptosystem by choosing $p$ and $q$ so that $a_p = a_q = 0$.

## 4. Attacks on RSA and its variations

**4.1. The GCD attack.** At the rump session of Crypto '95, Franklin and Reiter [25] identified a new attack against RSA with public exponent 3. Later, it was extended for exponents up to $\simeq 32$ bits by Patarin [57]. If two linearly dependent messages are encrypted with the same RSA cryptosystem, then it is possible to recover them as follows.

Let $m_1$ and $m_2 = m_1 + \Delta$ be the two messages, and let $c_1 = m_1^e \mod n$ and $c_2 = m_2^e \mod n$ be the corresponding ciphertexts. Then, let us form the polynomials $\mathcal{P}$ and $\mathcal{Q} \in \mathbb{Z}_n[x]$, defined by

$$(4.1) \qquad \mathcal{P}(x) = x^e - c_1 \pmod{n} \quad \text{and} \quad \mathcal{Q}(x) = (x + \Delta)^e - c_2 \pmod{n}.$$

Since the message $m_1$ is a root of $\mathcal{P}$ and $\mathcal{Q}$, $m_1$ will be a root of $\gcd(\mathcal{P}, \mathcal{Q})$ which is, with a high probability, a polynomial of degree 1. Solving this polynomial in $x$ gives the value of $m_1$, and $m_2 = m_1 + \Delta$. This attack was later generalized to any known polynomial relation between the messages and to any number of messages [14].

On the other hand, by expressing Lucas sequences as Dickson polynomials [49], Joye and Quisquater [34] proved the same result for LUC. Using division polynomials [66, Chap. 3, exercice 3.7], they also extended this attack to the KMOV and Demytko cryptosystems. Since the polynomial relation is of order $e^2$ for elliptic curves systems [34], the attack applies for public exponent up to $\simeq 16$ bits, instead of 32 bits as for RSA and LUC.

Furthermore, by lattice basis reduction techniques [48], Coppersmith [13] showed that if $\Delta$ (the difference between the two messages) is unknown, then $m_1$ and $m_2$ can sometimes be recovered. In fact, let $\varrho(\Delta)$ be the resultant in $x$ of $\mathcal{P}$ and $\mathcal{Q}$, which is an univariate polynomial in $\Delta$. It is possible to solve this polynomial $\varrho$ if the solution $\Delta$ is smaller than $n^{1/k}$, where $n$ is the public modulus and $k$ is the degree of $\varrho$. Since $k = e^2$ for RSA and LUC, and $k = e^4$ for elliptic curves system, KMOV and Demytko's cryptosystems tolerate smaller random padding.

**4.2. The common modulus attack.** Since RSA is multiplicative, the knowledge of two ciphertexts $c_1 = m^{e_1} \mod n$ and $c_2 = m^{e_2} \mod n$ of the message $m$ enables to recover message $m$, if the same modulus $n$ is used and if the public encryption keys $e_1$ and $e_2$ are relatively prime. Indeed, since $\gcd(e_1, e_2) = 1$, by the extended Euclidean algorithm [38], there exists $r, s \in \mathbb{Z}$ such that

$$(4.2) \qquad re_1 + se_2 = 1.$$

Consequently, we have

$$(4.3) \qquad m = m^{re_1 + se_2} = c_1^r c_2^s \mod n.$$

This was first noticed by Simmons [68].

KMOV is also homomorphic and is therefore susceptible to the same attack. This is not the case for LUC and Demytko's system. However, Bleichenbacher, Bosma and Lenstra [5] presented a signature forgery against LUC that requires two chosen signatures. Kaliski [36] established the same result for the Demytko's system. In his PhD. thesis, Bleichenbacher [3] shows how to forge a LUC signature from only *one* other signature. This was later adapted to Demytko's system [6]. This enables to exhibit the common modulus protocol failure as follows. We shall only illustrate the attack on LUC and refer to [6] for the attack on Demytko's system.

Let $(e_1, d_1)$ and $(e_2, d_2)$ be two pairs of encryption/decryption keys and let $n$ be the public modulus. Assuming $e_1$ relatively prime to $e_2$, let us use the extended Euclidean algorithm to find integers $r$ and $s$ such that $re_1 + se_2 = 1$. From the two ciphertexts $c_1 = V_{e_1}(m, 1) \bmod n$ and $c_2 = V_{e_2}(m, 1) \bmod n$, we find the message $m$ by

$$(4.4) \qquad m = \frac{1}{2} V_r(c_1, 1) V_s(c_2, 1) + \frac{c_1^2 - 4}{2} U_r(c_1, 1) U_s(c_2, 1) \frac{U_{e_2}(c_1, 1)}{U_{e_1}(c_2, 1)} \bmod n.$$

PROOF. From (2.7) and (2.3), it follows

$$\begin{aligned} U_{e_2}(c_1, 1) &= U_{e_2 e_1 d_1}(c_1, 1) \equiv U_{e_2 d_1}(c_1, 1) U_{e_1}(V_{e_2 d_1}(c_1, 1), 1) \\ &\equiv U_{e_2 d_1}(c_1, 1) U_{e_1}(c_2, 1) \pmod{n}. \end{aligned}$$

Hence,

$$\begin{aligned} 2m &\equiv 2V_{d_1}(c_1, 1) \equiv 2V_{d_1(re_1 + se_2)}(c_1, 1) \equiv V_{r + d_1 se_2}(c_1, 1) \\ &\equiv V_r(c_1, 1) V_{d_1 se_2}(c_1, 1) + \Delta U_r(c_1, 1) U_{d_1 se_2}(c_1, 1) \\ &\equiv V_r(c_1, 1) V_s(c_2, 1) + \Delta U_r(c_1, 1) U_{d_1 e_2}(c_1, 1) U_s(V_{d_1 e_2}(c_1, 1), 1) \\ &\equiv V_r(c_1, 1) V_s(c_2, 1) + (c_1^2 - 4) U_r(c_1, 1) U_{d_1 e_2}(c_1, 1) U_s(c_2, 1) \pmod{n}. \end{aligned}$$

$\square$

**4.3. The Wiener's attack.** Wiener [74] pointed out that if the secret key $d$ was chosen too small, then it might be recovered. He observed that when writing $ed = 1 + \frac{k}{g}(p-1)(q-1)$ with $\gcd(k, g) = 1$, we have

$$(4.5) \qquad \frac{k}{dg} - \frac{e}{n} = \frac{k}{dg}\left(\frac{1}{p} + \frac{1}{q} - \frac{1}{n}\right) - \frac{1}{dn}.$$

Following the presentation of Pinch [58], the attack of Wiener can be illustrated as follows.

THEOREM 4.1 ([28, p. 153]). *If $\left|\frac{a}{b} - x\right| < \frac{1}{2b^2}$, then $\frac{a}{b}$ is a continued fraction approximant for $x$.* $\square$

So, if the condition of the previous theorem is fulfilled, then $k/(dg)$ is a continued approximant for $e/n$. Since $e/n$ is public and since continued fractions can easily be computed, it is possible to find the secret exponent $d$ under certain assumptions. More precisely, Wiener proved the following corollary.

COROLLARY 4.2 ([74]). *Assume that $p \sim q \sim \sqrt{n}$, that $g = 2$ and that $e \sim n$. Then, $k \sim dg$ and the continued fraction attack will succeed for secret exponents of order up to $n^{1/4}$.* $\square$

Later, Pinch [58] proved the same result for the LUC and KMOV cryptosystems. He also extended this attack to Demytko's cryptosystem by using Theorem 3.3, and proved that the attack will succeed for secret exponents of order at most $n^{1/8}$.

## 5. Concluding remarks

The security of RSA-type systems are based on the difficulty of factoring the public modulus $n$. Against polynomial attacks, LUC presents no advantage comparatively to RSA because the degree of the polynomial is the same. This is not the case for elliptic curves RSA systems, where the degree is squared. Multiplicative-like attacks on LUC and KMOV/Demytko's system are not as general as for RSA, since the messages are precisely related. However, in some cases, they offer no advantage as in the common modulus failure, for example.

As mentioned in the introduction, the last type of attacks cannot really be considered as an attack. If the parameters are carefully chosen, RSA-type cryptosystems are considered to be secure.

Although Lucas based or elliptic curves based implementations are more time-consuming, they may offer some advantages in terms of security. Unfortunately, we cannot give a definitive answer to "What is the best RSA-type cryptosystem?". Given the state of the art, only the application will enable to choose the most adequate cryptosystem.

## Acknowledgments

We are very grateful to Daniel Bleichenbacher for fruitful discussions. Michael Merritt was also helpful in encouraging us to write this paper.

## References

[1] H. Aly and W. B. Müller, *Cryptosystems based on Dickson polynomials*, Presented at Pragocrypt '96, Prague, Czech Rep., 30 Sept-3 Oct. 1996.

[2] F. Bao, R. Deng, Y. Han, A. Jeng, A. D. Narasimhalu, and T.-H. Ngair, *Breaking public key cryptosystems on tamper resistant devices in the presence of transient faults*, Pre-proceedings of the 1997 Workshop on Security Protocols, Paris, France, 7-9th April 1997

[3] D. Bleichenbacher, *Efficiency and security analysis of cryptosystems based on number theory*, Ph.D. thesis, Swiss Federal Institute of Technology Zürich, 1996.

[4] _____, *On the security of the KMOV public key cryptosystem*, To appear in the proceedings of Crypto '97.

[5] D. Bleichenbacher, W. Bosma, and A. K. Lenstra, *Some remarks on Lucas-based cryptosystems*, Advances in Cryptology – Crypto '95 (D. Coppersmith, ed.), Lecture Notes in Computer Science, vol. 963, Springer-Verlag, 1995, pp. 386–396.

[6] D. Bleichenbacher, M. Joye, and J.-J. Quisquater, *A new and optimal chosen message attack on RSA-type cryptosystems*, Unpublished manuscript.

[7] D. Boneh, R. A. DeMillo, and R. J. Lipton, *On the importance of checking cryptographic protocols for faults*, Advances in Cryptology – Eurocrypt '97 (W. Fumy, ed.), Lecture Notes in Computer Science, vol. 1233, Springer-Verlag, 1997, pp. 37–51.

[8] D. M. Bressoud, *Factorization and primality testing*, Undergraduate Texts in Mathematics, Springer-Verlag, 1989.

[9] L. S. Charlap and D. P. Robbins, *An elementary introduction to elliptic curves*, CRD Expository Report No. 31, Institute for Defense Analysis, Princeton, December 1988.

[10] H. Cohen, *A course in computational algebraic number theory*, Graduate Texts in Mathematics, vol. 138, Springer-Verlag, 1993.

[11] D. Coppersmith, *Small solutions to polynomials equations, and low exponent RSA vulnerabilities*, Submitted to *Journal of Cryptology*.

[12] _____, *Finding a small root of a bivariate integer equation; factoring with high bits known*, Advances in Cryptology – Eurocrypt '96 (U. Maurer, ed.), Lecture Notes in Computer Science, vol. 1070, Springer-Verlag, 1996, pp. 178–189.

[13] _____, *Finding a small root of a univariate modular equation*, Advances in Cryptology – Eurocrypt '96 (U. Maurer, ed.), Lecture Notes in Computer Science, vol. 1070, Springer-Verlag, 1996, pp. 155–165.

[14] D. Coppersmith, M. Franklin, J. Patarin, and M. Reiter, *Low exponent RSA with related messages*, Advances in Cryptology – Eurocrypt '96 (U. Maurer, ed.), Lecture Notes in Computer Science, vol. 1070, Springer-Verlag, 1996, pp. 1–9.

[15] G. Davida, *Chosen signature cryptanalysis of the RSA (MIT) public key cryptosystem*, Tech. Report TR-CS-82-2, Dept. of Electrical Engineering and Computer Science, University of Wisconsin, Milwaukee, USA, October 1982.

[16] W. de Jonge and D. Chaum, *Attacks on some RSA signatures*, Advances in Cryptology – Crypto '85 (H. C. Williams, ed.), Lecture Notes in Computer Science, vol. 218, Springer-Verlag, 1986, pp. 18–27.

[17] J. M. DeLaurentis, *A further weakness in the common modulus protocol for the RSA cryptoalgorithm*, Cryptologia **8** (1984), no. 3, 253–259.

[18] R. DeMillo, N. A. Lynch, and M. J. Merritt, *Cryptographic protocols*, Proc. SIGACT Conf., 1982.

[19] R. A. Demillo and M. J. Merrit, *Chosen signatures cryptanalysis of public key cryptosystems*, Technical memorandum, School of Information and Computer Science, Georgia Institute of Technology, Atlanta, Georgia 30322, October 1982.

[20] N. Demytko, *A new elliptic curve based analogue of RSA*, Advances in Cryptology – Eurocrypt '93 (T. Helleseth, ed.), Lecture Notes in Computer Science, vol. 765, Springer-Verlag, 1994, pp. 40–49.

[21] D. E. Denning, *Digital signatures with RSA and other public-key cryptosystems*, Communications of the ACM **27** (1984), no. 4, 388–392.

[22] Y. Desmedt and A. M. Odlyzko, *A chosen text attack on the RSA cryptosystem and some discrete logarithms schemes*, Advances in Cryptology – Crypto '85 (H. C. Williams, ed.), Lecture Notes in Computer Science, vol. 218, Springer-Verlag, 1986, pp. 516–521.

[23] W. Diffie and M. E. Hellman, *New directions in cryptography*, IEEE Transactions on Information Theory **IT-26** (1976), no. 6, 644–654.

[24] T. ElGamal, *A public key cryptosystem and a signature scheme based on discrete logarithms*, IEEE Transactions on Information Theory **IT-31** (1985), no. 4, 469–472.

[25] M. K. Franklin and M. K. Reiter, *A linear protocol failure for RSA with exponent three*, Preliminary note for *Crypto '95* rump session.

[26] M. Girault and J.-F. Misarski, *Selective forgery of RSA signatures using redundancy*, Advances in Cryptology – Eurocrypt '97 (W. Fumy, ed.), Lecture Notes in Computer Science, vol. 1233, Springer-Verlag, 1997, pp. 493–507.

[27] L. C. Guillou, J.-J. Quisquater, M. Walker, P. Landrock, and C. Shaer, *Precautions taken against various potential attacks*, Advances in Cryptology – Eurocrypt '90 (I. B. Damgård, ed.), Lecture Notes in Computer Science, vol. 473, Springer-Verlag, 1991, pp. 465–473.

[28] G. H. Hardy and E. M. Wright, *An introduction to the theory of numbers*, 5th ed., Oxford University Press, 1979.

[29] J. Håstad, *On using RSA with low exponent in a public key network*, Advances in Cryptology – Crypto '85 (H. C. Williams, ed.), Lecture Notes in Computer Science, vol. 218, Springer-Verlag, 1986, pp. 404–408.

[30] _____, *Solving simultaneous modular equations of low degree*, SIAM J. Comput. **17** (1988), no. 2, 336–341.

[31] D. Husemöller, *Elliptic curves*, Graduate Texts in Mathematics, vol. 111, Springer-Verlag, 1987.

[32] M. Joye, A. K. Lenstra, and J.-J. Quisquater, *Chinese remaindering in the presence of faults*, Submitted to Journal of Cryptology.

[33] M. Joye and J.-J. Quisquater, *On the importance of securing your bins: The garbage-man-in-the-middle attack*, Proc. of the 4th ACM Conference on Computer and Communications Security (T. Matsumoto, ed.), ACM Press, 1997, pp. 135–141.

[34] _____, *Protocol failures for RSA-like functions using Lucas sequences and elliptic curves*, Security Protocols (M. Lomas, ed.), Lecture Notes in Computer Science, vol. 1189, Springer-Verlag, 1997, pp. 93–100.

[35] B. S. Kaliski Jr, *Elliptic curves and cryptography: A pseudorandom bit generator and other tools*, Ph.D. thesis, Massachusetts Institute of Technology, 1988.

[36] _____, *A chosen message attack on Demytko's elliptic curve cryptosystem*, Journal of Cryptology **10** (1997), no. 1, 71–72.

[37] A. Knapp, *Elliptic curves*, Mathematical Notes, Princeton University Press, 1992.

[38] D. E. Knuth, *The art of computer programming: Volume 2/seminumerical algorithms*, 2nd ed., Addison-Wesley Publishing Company, 1981.
[39] N. Koblitz, *Elliptic curve cryptosystems*, Mathematics of Computation **48** (1987), 203–209.
[40] _____, *A course in number theory and cryptography*, 2nd ed., Graduate Texts in Mathematics, vol. 114, Springer-Verlag, 1994.
[41] K. Koyama, U. M. Maurer, T. Okamoto, and S. A. Vanstone, *New public-key schemes based on elliptic curves over the ring $\mathbb{Z}_n$*, Advances in Cryptology – Crypto'91 (J. Feigenbaum, ed.), Lecture Notes in Computer Science, vol. 576, Springer-Verlag, 1991, pp. 252–266.
[42] K. Kurosawa, K. Okada, and S. Tsujii, *Low exponent attack against elliptic curve RSA*, Advances in Cryptology – Asiacrypt'94 (J. Pieprzyk and R. Safavi-Naini, eds.), Lecture Notes in Computer Science, vol. 917, Springer-Verlag, 1995, pp. 376–383.
[43] H. Kuwakado and K. Koyama, *Security of RSA-type cryptosystems over elliptic curves against Håstad attack*, Electronics Letters **30** (1994), no. 22, 123–124.
[44] C.-S. Laih, F.-K. Tu, and W.-C. Tai, *Remarks on LUC public key system*, Electronics Letters **30** (1994), no. 2, 123–124.
[45] C.-S. Laih, F.-K. Tu, and W.-C. Tai, *On the security of the Lucas functions*, Informations Processing Letters **53** (1995), 243–247.
[46] S. Lang, *Elliptic curves: Diophantine analysis*, Grundlehren der mathematischen Wissenschaften, vol. 231, Springer-Verlag, 1978.
[47] A. K. Lenstra, *Memo on RSA signature generation in the presence of faults*, September 1996.
[48] A. K. Lenstra, H. W. Lenstra Jr, and L. Lovasz, *Factoring polynomials with integer coefficients*, Matematische Annalen **261** (1982), 513–534.
[49] R. Lidl, G. L. Mullen, and G. Turnwald, *Dickson polynomials*, Longman Scientific & Technical, 1993.
[50] A. J. Menezes, *Elliptic curve public key cryptosystems*, Kluwer Academic Publishers, 1993.
[51] V. S. Miller, *Use of elliptic curves in cryptography*, Advances in Cryptology – Crypto'85 (H. C. Williams, ed.), Lecture Notes in Computer Science, vol. 218, Springer-Verlag, 1986, pp. 417–426.
[52] P. L. Montgomery, *Speeding the Pollard and elliptic curve methods of factorization*, Mathematics of Computation **48** (1987), no. 177, 243–264.
[53] J. H. Moore, *Protocol failures in cryptosystems*, Contemporary Cryptology (G. Simmons, ed.), IEEE Press, 1992, pp. 541–558.
[54] W. B. Müller and R. Nöbauer, *Some remarks on public-key cryptosystems*, Sci. Math. Hungar **16** (1981), 71–76.
[55] _____, *Cryptanalysis of the Dickson scheme*, Advances in Cryptology – Eurocrypt'85 (J. Pichler, ed.), Lecture Notes in Computer Science, vol. 219, Springer-Verlag, 1986, pp. 50–61.
[56] S. Murphy, *Remarks on the LUC public key system*, Electronics Letters **30** (1994), no. 7, 558–559.
[57] J. Patarin, *Some serious protocol failures for RSA with exponent e of less than $\simeq 32$ bits*, Presented at the conference of cryptography, CIRM Luminy, France, September 1995.
[58] R. G. E. Pinch, *Extending the Håstad attack to LUC*, Electronics Letters **31** (1995), no. 21, 1827–1828.
[59] _____, *Extending the Wiener attack to RSA-type cryptosystems*, Electronics Letters **31** (1995), no. 20, 1736–1738.
[60] M. O. Rabin, *Digital signatures and public-key functions as intractable as factorization*, Tech. Report MIT/LCS/TR-212, MIT Laboratory for Computer Science, January 1979.
[61] P. Ribenboim, *The little book of big primes*, Springer-Verlag, 1991.
[62] H. Riesel, *Prime numbers and computer methods for factorization*, Progress in Mathematics, vol. 57, Birkhäuser, 1985.
[63] R. L. Rivest, A. Shamir, and L. Adleman, *A method for obtaining digital signatures and public-key cryptosystems*, Communications of the ACM **21** (1978), no. 2, 120–126.
[64] R. Schoof, *Elliptic curves over finite fields and the computation of square roots mod p*, Mathematics of Computation **44** (1985), no. 170, 483–494.
[65] A. Shamir, *A fast signature scheme*, Tech. Report MIT/LCS/TM-107, MIT Lab. for Computer Science, Cambridge, Mass., July 1978.
[66] J. H. Silverman, *The arithmetic of elliptic curves*, Graduate Texts in Mathematics, vol. 106, Springer-Verlag, 1986.

[67] J. H. Silverman and J. Tate, *Rational points on elliptic curves*, Undergraduate Texts in Mathematics, Springer-Verlag, 1992.
[68] G. J. Simmons, *A 'weak' privacy protocol using the RSA crypto algorithm*, Cryptologia **7** (1983), no. 2, 180–182.
[69] A. Smith and C. Boyd, *An elliptic curve analogue of McCurley's key agreement scheme*, Cryptography and Coding (C. Boyd, ed.), Lecture Notes in Computer Science, vol. 1025, Springer-Verlag, 1995, pp. 150–157.
[70] P. Smith, *LUC public-key encryption*, Dr. Dobb's Journal (1993), 44–49.
[71] P. Smith and C. Skinner, *A public-key cryptosystem and a digital signature based on the Lucas function analogue to discrete logarithms*, Advances in Cryptology – Asiacrypt '94 (J. Pieprzyk, ed.), Lecture Notes in Computer Science, vol. 917, Springer-Verlag, 1995, pp. 357–364.
[72] P. J. Smith and M. J. J. Lennon, *LUC: A new public key system*, Ninth IFIP Symposium on Computer Security (E. G. Douglas, ed.), Elsevier Science Publishers, 1993, pp. 103–117.
[73] T. Takagi and S. Naito, *The multi-variable modular polynomial and its applications to cryptography*, 7th International Symposium on Algorithm and Computation, ISAAC'96, Lecture Notes in Computer Science, vol. 1178, 1996, pp. 386–396.
[74] M. J. Wiener, *Cryptanalysis of short RSA secret exponents*, IEEE Transactions on Information Theory **36** (1990), no. 3, 553–558.
[75] H. C. Williams, *A modification of the RSA public-key encryption procedure*, IEEE Transactions on Information Theory **IT-26** (1980), no. 6, 726–729.

UCL Crypto Group, Dép. de Mathématique, Université catholique de Louvain, Chemin du Cyclotron 2, B-1348 Louvain-la-Neuve, Belgium
  *E-mail address*: joye@agel.ucl.ac.be
  *URL*: http://www.dice.ucl.ac.be/crypto/joye/

UCL Crypto Group, Lab. de Micro-électronique, Université catholique de Louvain, Place du Levant 3, B-1348 Louvain-la-Neuve, Belgium
  *E-mail address*: jjq@dice.ucl.ac.be
  *URL*: http://www.dice.ucl.ac.be/crypto/jjq.html

# Information Leakage in Encrypted Key Exchange

Sarvar Patel

ABSTRACT. Encrypted Key Exchange(EKE) protocol promises to protect against off-line dictionary attacks on passwords, as long as we are careful about avoiding information leakage. EKE presents a form of random padding as a way to avoid leakage in exact and large blocks. We show this method to be ineffective for exact blocks and for large blocks we show the method to be effective only with sufficiently large blocks. We also present another method and analyze both methods. Furthermore we present a general framework to transfer under encryption difficult numbers, like primes, without leaking information about the password.

## 1. Introduction

A random key along with a secure protocol provides the best method of authentication over an insecure network. Unfortunately, humans cannot remember random keys. One of the greatest network threats is also one of the oldest: Bad passwords allow an eavesdropper to mount an off-line dictionary attack. For example, when an eavesdropper listens for a challenge $R$ and the password encrypted response $P(R)$, then, off-line, the eavesdropper encrypts $R$ with all passwords in the dictionary and compares the result with $P(R)$. If one of the passwords in the dictionary matches, then the secret password has been discovered.

Bellovin and Merrit [1] have presented interesting and novel protocols which are secure not only against active attacks, but also against off-line dictionary attacks. Information leakage, which allows one to eliminate password choices, is tricky to avoid in these protocols. The authors suggest a way of random padding to block information leakage. We show this method to be generally ineffective and the problem of leakage to be more subtle. Unless the leakage problem is addressed, these protocols have limited use as protection against off-line dictionary attacks. We recommend a way not of eliminating leakage, but of keeping it in check. In fact, we can reduce leakage to an extent that off-line attacks are no better than on-line ones. We also present ways to transfer under encryption difficult numbers, like prime numbers, with out leaking any information about the password used to encrypt the prime. We also present a general framework where numbers of particular characteristics can be transferred without leakage.

EKE uses public-key and secret-key cryptography allowing a user and a server, sharing a password, to authenticate and exchange information over an insecure network. EKE has variants using RSA, Diffie-Hellman Exchange, and ElGamal.

---

1991 *Mathematics Subject Classification*. Primary 94A60, 68P25; Secondary 68Q99.

```
Alice                                  Bob
  |                                     |
1 |         Alice, n, P(e)              |
  |------------------------------------>|
2 |         P(R^e mod n)                |
  |<------------------------------------|
  |                                     |
3 |             R(C_A)                  |
  |------------------------------------>|
4 |           R(C_A, C_B)               |
  |<------------------------------------|
5 |             R(C_B)                  |
  |------------------------------------>|
```

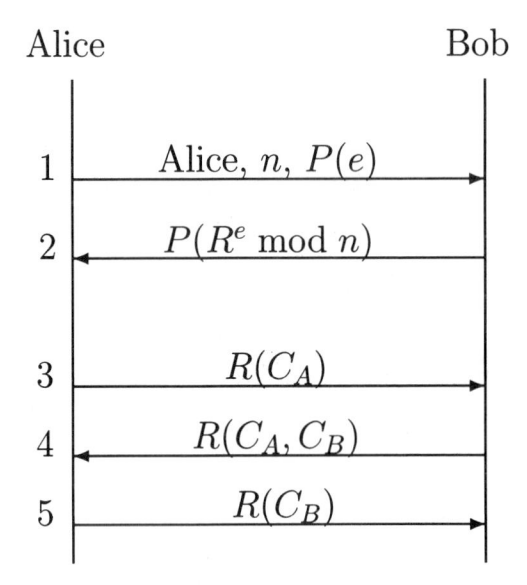

FIGURE 1. EKE using RSA

The RSA version of EKE is sketched in Figure 1. In step 1 of the RSA scheme, Alice generates a random public key $e$ and the corresponding private key $d$. Alice transfers the public key to Bob by encrypting it in a secret-key cryptosystem using the password $P$. Bob responds by generating a random session key $R$ and encrypts it using the public key, which in turn is further encrypted using the password $P$. The rest of the steps are standard exchanges of challenges $C_A$ and $C_B$ to authenticate session key $R$. An eavesdropper listening to the exchanges has no easy way to validate password guesses. The only way to validate the guesses is to break the public key system (For some number theoretic attacks without breaking the public key system, see [3]).

Similarly, key exchange in the Diffie-Hellman (see Figure 2) is encrypted using password $P$ to protect against a 'man in the middle' attack. Also, an eavesdropper cannot validate password guesses because $R_A$ and $R_B$ are random hence $g^{R_A} \mod p$ and $g^{R_B} \mod p$ will also appear random. Furthermore, even if they are correctly guessed, there is no way to calculate the session key $K = g^{R_A R_B} \mod p$. However, Alice can calculate session key $K$ by raising the received $g^{R_B} \mod p$ to known $R_A$. In the rest of the steps, challenges are sent to validate the session key $K$.

## 2. Information Leakage

**2.1. Large Block.** Suppose we are using password $P$ to encrypt numbers mod a prime $p$, but the block size of the system is larger than $p$, in fact many multiples of $p$. Now, an attacker can use password guesses $P'$ from a dictionary and try to decrypt for example $P(g^{R_A} \mod p)$. If the decryption results in a number greater than $p$ then that password guess $P'$ can be rejected. Thus some information is leaking, similarly all passwords in the dictionary can be tried and those resulting in decryption greater than $p$ will be rejected. Then more encryptions from other sessions can be used to narrow the viable passwords in the dictionary down to one.

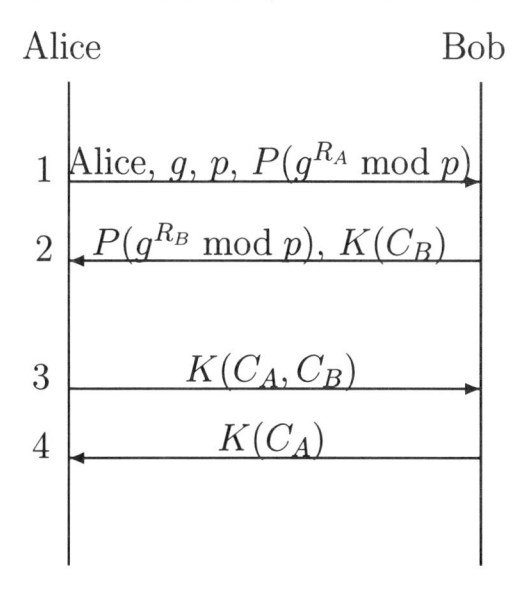

```
                Alice                        Bob
                  |                           |
               1  |Alice, g, p, P(g^{R_A} mod p)|
                  |-------------------------->|
               2  |  P(g^{R_B} mod p), K(C_B) |
                  |<--------------------------|
                  |                           |
                  |                           |
               3  |        K(C_A, C_B)        |
                  |-------------------------->|
               4  |          K(C_A)           |
                  |<--------------------------|
                  |                           |
```

FIGURE 2. EKE using Diffie Hellman

**2.2. Exact Block.** Even if the block size does not have more bits than that required to code a number of length $p$, information leakage is still possible. Let us say that if $n$ bits are the minimum required to code $p$ then that leaves us with $2^n - p$ numbers greater than $p$, and all password guesses whose decryptions yield these numbers can be rejected.

## 3. Random Padding

**3.1. Simple Padding.** In large blocks the higher bits, not necessary to represent $p$, cannot be trivially set to all zeroes because this will allow the attacker to validate passwords. One simple way of padding is to set the high bits to a random value. Now, an attacker could not validate a trial password because any value in the high bits might have been randomly set before encryption. This is not entirely true because the vulnerabilities of an exact block are still with us. We have just made leakage in a large block no worse than an exact block because if $n$ bits are the minimum required to code $p$, that leaves us with $2^n - p$ numbers greater than $p$, and all password guesses whose decryptions yield these numbers can be rejected.

**3.2. EKE Padding.** The authors in [1] suggest a way to deal with the problem in exact blocks and large blocks simultaneously by randomly adding multiples of $p$ to the number, so that all numbers are possible, and the receiver can always remove the random adding by performing mod $p$. In Diffie-Hellman key exchange the random adding should make no difference in calculating the session key. If $m$ is the size of the block then $2^m$ numbers are possible. Let $x = \lfloor \frac{2^m}{p} \rfloor$ and the remainder $r = 2^m \bmod p$. If the input is less than $r$ then pick a random $0 \leq j \leq x$ and add $jp$ to input. If the input is between $r$ and $p$ then pick random $j$, $0 \leq j \leq x - 1$ and add $jp$ to input.

## 4. Leakage in EKE Padding

Unfortunately, there is a weakness in this method of EKE padding which can under certain conditions allow significant leakage. Not only must the random padding method make all numbers possible under decryption, but it must also make the probability of all numbers the same. Unmodified, the above method does not guarantee equal distribution. It is susceptible to a modified off-line dictionary attack.

**4.1. Modified Dictionary Attack.** First we collect encryptions from many sessions, then for each password guess from the dictionary, we keep a coarse histogram of the occurrence of ranges of numbers. So instead of rejecting a subset of passwords after each session encryption, we now count occurrences of numbers in some ranges. When we see that a distribution is not uniformly distributed, then we try an on-line attack for that password guess. Eventually we will be successful, but much sooner than a brute force on-line attack.

**4.2. Leakage in an Exact Block.** We will present an example to motivate. Assume that only one interval of $p$ completely fits in $2^m$. At the two end intervals a) 0 to $r = (2^m \bmod p)$ and b) $p$ to $2^m$, the probability distribution due to EKE padding is not uniform. Assuming uniformity we would expect $\frac{2r}{2^m}$ numbers to fall in those intervals. However, due to EKE padding, we now expect $\frac{r}{p}$ numbers to fall in those intervals. Assuming $r$ is about $\frac{p}{2}$, then we expect randomly about $\frac{2}{3}$ of the numbers to fall in the two ends. With EKE padding we expect only $\frac{1}{2}$ of the numbers to fall in the two ends. A modified dictionary attack can easily exploit such difference.

**4.3. Leakage in Large Blocks.** We define $f$, to be the ratio $\frac{r}{p}$ such that $0 < f < 1$. In EKE padding, the numbers that fall in to all the sections composed of the first r numbers in each multiple p are equal to $\frac{r}{p} = f$. In a uniform prime scheme, the numbers that fall in to all the sections are $(X+1)r$. Hence the fraction that fall in the sections is $\frac{(X+1)r}{2^m} = \frac{f(X+1)}{(X+f)}$. As examples in Figure 3, 4, 5, we give a list of different $f$ with different $X$ and what fraction of numbers actually end up falling in those sections. The greater the difference between the the EKE padding column and the uniform distribution column the easier it is to discover the password. Different values of $f$ means different number of extra bits are needed to fit $X$ of them in the large block.

## 5. Set-High-Bits Method

Picking prime number $p$ arbitrarily close to $2^m$ is another method of reducing information leakage [1]. In this method, while picking prime $p$, we set certain number of high bits to one. Also, if we have a larger block, we set the high bits to one and then pick a prime by randomly trying lower bits till one passes a primality test. We will pick $k$ such bits, with higher $k$ giving us less information leakage. The only way to invalidate a password guess is if the decryption of a session encryption results in 1s at all high $k$ bits and the number formed by the remaining $m-k$ bits is greater than the number formed by the lower $m-k$ bits in prime $p$. The chance of that happening is less than $\frac{1}{2^k}$.

We would like to pick $k$ such that to mount an off-line attack an attacker would need to hear or carry out as many sessions as in mounting a direct on-line

# INFORMATION LEAKAGE IN ENCRYPTED KEY EXCHANGE

| Extra bits needed $= \lceil X(1-f) \rceil$ | $X$ | EKE Padding distribution= $f$ | Uniform distribution $= \frac{f(X+1)}{(X+f)}$ |
|---|---|---|---|
| 1 | 1 | 0.100000 | 0.181818 |
| 4 | 4 | 0.100000 | 0.121951 |
| 9 | 10 | 0.100000 | 0.108911 |
| 15 | 16 | 0.100000 | 0.105590 |
| 18 | 22 | 0.100000 | 0.104072 |
| 31 | 34 | 0.100000 | 0.102639 |
| 45 | 49 | 0.100000 | 0.101833 |
| 55 | 61 | 0.100000 | 0.101473 |
| 58 | 64 | 0.100000 | 0.101404 |

FIGURE 3. Total Numbers Falling in Intervals of Length $r$ with $f = 0.1$

| Extra bits needed $= \lceil X(1-f) \rceil$ | $X$ | EKE Padding distribution= $f$ | Uniform distribution $= \frac{f(X+1)}{(X+f)}$ |
|---|---|---|---|
| 1 | 1 | 0.300000 | 0.461538 |
| 3 | 4 | 0.300000 | 0.348837 |
| 7 | 10 | 0.300000 | 0.320388 |
| 12 | 16 | 0.300000 | 0.312883 |
| 16 | 22 | 0.300000 | 0.309417 |
| 24 | 34 | 0.300000 | 0.306122 |
| 35 | 49 | 0.300000 | 0.30426 |
| 43 | 61 | 0.300000 | 0.303426 |
| 45 | 64 | 0.300000 | 0.303266 |

FIGURE 4. Total Numbers Falling in Intervals of Length $r$ with $f = 0.3$

| Extra bits needed $= \lceil X(1-f) \rceil$ | $X$ | EKE Padding distribution= $f$ | Uniform distribution $= \frac{f(X+1)}{(X+f)}$ |
|---|---|---|---|
| 1 | 1 | 0.500000 | 0.666667 |
| 2 | 4 | 0.500000 | 0.555556 |
| 5 | 10 | 0.500000 | 0.523810 |
| 8 | 16 | 0.500000 | 0.515152 |
| 11 | 22 | 0.500000 | 0.511111 |
| 17 | 34 | 0.500000 | 0.507246 |
| 25 | 49 | 0.500000 | 0.505051 |
| 31 | 61 | 0.500000 | 0.504065 |
| 32 | 64 | 0.500000 | 0.503876 |

FIGURE 5. Total Numbers Falling in Intervals of Length $r$ with $f = 0.5$

attack. We will call this the off-line/on-line threshold bits, $T$. In calculating $T$, we assume the best case for the attacker that $\frac{1}{2^k} N_P$ are rejected then at next iteration $(1 - \frac{1}{2^k}) N_P$ are left where $N_P$ are the number of passwords in the dictionary. Since we want to terminate after $i$ iterations when only one password is left we have the equation, $1 = (1 - \frac{1}{2^k})^i N_P$. Since we want to require $N_P$ iterations, the same as in off-line attack, we substitute $N_P$ for $i$ and solve for $k$ or $T$ bits, $T = \lg(\frac{1}{1 - 2^{-\frac{\lg N_P}{N_P}}})$. As an example, for $N_P = 1000,000$, the high $T = 16$ bits have to be 1, to require the same number of iterations from an off-line attack as required by an on-line attack.

A similar analysis is presented in [2], but only assuming that the attacker can eavesdrop on legitimate sessions. We on the other hand have assumed the attacker can query legitimate users and use responses in ruling out passwords. There is an obvious, but unsatisfying, defense against such an attacker. A machine can limit the number of consecutive unsuccessful tries and upon reaching that limit lock out the account. The attacker can try to evade such requirements by interleaving their unsuccessful sessions with successful sessions carried by legitimate users. Setting an overall limit may make denial of service attacks much easier.

Nevertheless, even with such limits $T$, the off-line/on-line threshold, serves as an important measure because any more protection is useless. Setting more than $T$ bits to one will require the attacker to make more queries than the passwords in the dictionary. Then the attacker can move to the simple on-line attack of trying all passwords in the dictionary until the correct one is found.

## 6. Transferring Special Numbers Under Encryption

The authors of EKE [1] assume there is no way to encrypt special numbers like prime without leaking some information. We present a method which encrypts primes with little or no leakage. Furthermore, we show how in general to tackle special numbers. In order to encrypt a prime $p$, Alice should first find the next higher prime, by primality testing, and then A should pick a random number $j$ between them, and encrypt and transmit $j$. Bob upon receiving encrypted $j$ will decrypt it with the password $P$ and then will descend starting with $j$ until he finds a prime. Now when a attacker tries to decrypt with a guessed password, he is no wiser because all numbers have equal probability of occurring. Since primes are distributed by $\frac{1}{\ln N}$, so it is possible for the user to find them in a reasonable time.

In general, many special numbers can be encrypted by this method. First we need a test to verify whether a number satisfies the special predicate. Then we have to find the next number which also satisfies the predicate. Then we pick a random number from the range starting with the current predicate and ending right before the next predicate. For example, even when we try to hide odd numbers we basically follow the same scheme. First we find the next odd number, then we randomly pick the current number or the next even number because after that we have the next odd number. However, there may be some special numbers, like RSA number $n = pq$, for which there are no good tests unlike tests for odd and prime numbers.

### 6.1. Different Methods of Prime Generation.
We haven't so far mentioned the distribution of primes because we were only looking at the problem of transferring primes, independent of generation. However, some distributions leak more information and some less and some none. We will look at 3 typical schemes for generation that people use and what kind of leakage is possible.

In practice there are only few ways people generate primes:

**A:** pick a number, test for primality, if prime then stop else repeat.

**B:** pick a number $j$, test for primality, if prime then stop else try $j + 1$.

**C:** pick a number $j$, test for primality, if prime then stop else try $j - 1$.

**6.2. Different Methods of Transfer.** We have mentioned the 'going up method' of picking next prime $p^+$ and sending random $r$ between $p$ and $p^+$. Of course one could also have used a 'going down method' of picking previous prime $p^-$ and send $r$ between $p^-$ and $p$. This may also be generalizable to look at more than one neighboring prime and send $r$ as a function of them.

Let us define $pi(n)$ as number of primes less than $n$. Scheme A picks primes with equal probability $\frac{1}{pi(n)}$ and we call this the 'uniform prime' scheme. However scheme B picks prime $p$ with probability $\frac{(p-p^-)}{n}$ or $\frac{(dp^-)}{n}$ and C picks prime $p$ with probability $\frac{(p^+-p)}{n}$ or $\frac{dp^+}{n}$ and we refer to these schemes as 'uniform number' schemes. Now if you know the generation scheme then you can pick the appropriate going up or going down transfer method to keep the information leakage in check. In particular, if you know that scheme B is being used for generation then we can use the going down method and pick $r$ between $p^-$ and $p$ primes, and vice versa with scheme C. This way we know the primes are picked with distribution $\frac{dp}{n}$ and all numbers between 0 and $n$ are equally likely when we transfer. Thus primes can be encrypted without fear of leakage. This is why we refer to scheme A and B as 'uniform number' scheme because each number can have an equal likelihood of occurring which is not true in scheme A or the 'uniform prime' scheme. The distribution of primes, however, is not uniform in the 'uniform number' scheme.

**6.3. Simplified Method of Generation and Transfer.** If we assume that both generation and transference of the primes are in our control then we can use a more efficient scheme as suggested by David Wagner [4]. Alice simply picks a number $r$ and transfers it to Bob. Both Alice and Bob now test $r$ for primality. If $r$ is not prime then the next number is tried until a number passes the primality test. This number is the prime that will be used. Only one prime generation and one random number generation is needed on a user's part. This way all numbers prior to encryption are equally likely. However, the primes do not occur with uniform distribution, but rather depend upon the distance of the neighboring prime as in the 'uniform number' scheme.

**6.4. Some Leakage Possible in Uniform Prime Scheme.** Unfortunately in scheme A, where primes are uniformly generated, some leakage is possible because for a prime p, the numbers between $p$ and $p^+$ are not uniformly distributed [4]. However, it is practically impossible to see that they are not uniformly distributed because there are too many primes and it is virtually impossible that the same prime will be picked again at random, so one will never see enough $j$ between a given prime $p$ and successor $p^+$ to find out if they are uniformly distributed or not. For example, a 512 bit number has $\frac{2^{512}}{\ln 2^{512}}$ or about $2^{503}$ primes and the likelihood of a prime being repeated is virtually nil, let alone seeing that the $j$ are not uniformly distributed.

However there is a more powerful attack based on the distribution of $dp$ of different lengths. The lengths occur with different distribution in the 'uniform prime' scheme and the 'uniform number' scheme. So one can envision the numbers from 0 to $n$ separated by primes in to lengths of $dp(1)$, $dp(2)$,...$dp(i)$, $dp(i+1)$....,$dp(pi(n))$. Let us say $dp$ of length $l$ occur $N(l)$ times in numbers up to $n$. In 'uniform prime' scheme each $dp(i)$ is equally likely and the distribution of $l$, $f(l)$, is $\frac{N(l)}{pi(n)}$ or $\frac{(\ln n * N(l))}{n}$. Whereas in the 'uniform number' scheme the distribution of $l$, $g(l)$ is $\frac{l*N(l)}{n}$. So an attacker can for a particular password decrypt the numbers, find the neighboring primes, and note the length $l$. After collecting enough $l$ the attacker can see if the underlying distribution is more consistent with $f(l)$ or $g(l)$. So for small $l$ the 'uniform number' scheme will have a smaller probability than with the same $l$ in 'uniform prime' scheme. For larger $l$, the 'uniform number' scheme will have a larger probability than with the same $l$ in the 'uniform prime' scheme. For $l$ around $\ln n$ the distributions are similar. Since $l$ near $\ln n$ will dominate, it is not clear if we can estimate the difference. Basically the distribution of $l$ in 'uniform prime' gets moved to the right in the 'uniform number' scheme.

So two things have to occur, for even this attack to be successful, we have to know the distribution of $l$ at some level. Furthermore even if we know the distribution, it is not clear if we can detect the difference in distribution of $l$s and have information leaked. Even if we allow, say thousands of primes encrypted by a password to be observed by an attacker, it is not clear if that is enough to measure the small change of distribution of $l$s. Especially since most of the thousands of primes will yield $l$s near $\ln n$. So in general, to transfer special numbers with arbitrary distribution, we will have leakage, but this may be kept in check if either the moments or distributions of $f(l)$ or $g(l)$ are not known or the difference cannot be detected even given thousands of observations.

## 7. Conclusion

We have shown how information leakage is possible in the scheme outlined by the authors of EKE and that large padding is required to keep leakage in check. We present another scheme and show a way of keeping leakage in check to the point that off-line attacks become as burdensome as on-line attacks. Finally we show how apparently untransferable numbers, like primes, can be encrypted with leaking little or no information.

## 8. Acknowledgment

I want to thank David Wagner for his comments on a previous abstract version of the paper.

## References

[1] Steven Bellovin, and Michael Merritt, *Encrypted Key Exchange: Password-Based Protocols Secure Against Dictionary Attacks*, Proc. IEEE Computer Society Symposium on Research in Security and Privacy, May 1992.
[2] Barry Jaspan, *Dual-workfactor Encrypted Key Exchange: Efficiently Preventing Password Chaining and Dictionary Attacks*, The Sixth USENIX Security Symposium Proceedings, July 1996.
[3] Sarvar Patel, *Number Theoretic Attacks On Secure Password Schemes*, Proc. IEEE Symposium on Security and Privacy, May 1997.
[4] David Wagner, Personal Communication, 1996.
MATH AND CRYPTOGRAPHY RESEARCH GROUP, BELLCORE, MORRISTOWN, NEW JERSEY 07960
*E-mail address*: `sarvar@bellcore.com`

# Observed Weaknesses in Security Dynamics' Client/Server Protocol

## Adam Shostack

**Abstract**. *The protocol used by Security Dynamics in versions of their software prior to 1.3 has substantial flaws which appear to be exploitable and reduce the security of a system using Security Dynamics software to that of a username and password. In this paper, we explain the protocol in some detail, show the outline of how the attack would work, and offer some defenses against the attack. The attack has not yet been implemented. There do not seem to be easy defenses available within the current protocol — an upgrade is the best option. We also suggest some additional areas for future research.*

1991 Mathematics Subject Classification: Primary: 68M10, 68P25

© 1998 Adam Shostack

## I. Introduction

The SecurID system is a popular form of two factor authentication that involves a small handheld card distributed to users, client software for a variety of systems and server software for centralized authentication and management.

The card contains an 8 bit microprocessor, a clock, an LCD, a battery and possibly a pressure sensitive keypad. The unit is housed in a tamper resistant steel case, and is designed to erase its memory if opened. The card generates a stream of apparently unrelated numbers of fixed length (referred to as cardcodes) by combining a factory programmed seed with the time, and running those through what is commonly thought of as 'the' 'SecurID hash.' Security Dynamics actually has two hashes, the card hash and a second hash called F2. (See below for some details of F2.) The length of the cardcode can be from 6-8 digits, and does not vary for a given card. If the card has a keypad, the card can combine a PIN (of 4-8 digits, configurable by the administrator) with the output of the hash. The PIN is added to the output of the hash by no carry addition. If the card does not have a keypad, the user is expected to prepend his PIN to the cardcode when sending it to be authenticated. Security Dynamics has announced a software token, which is not considered here.

The client software consists of a modification to a host's authentication system so that it can communicate with an ACE/Server. Software exists for a wide variety of systems, from AppleTalk Remote Access to Cisco routers, Annex Terminal servers, and UNIX workstations. We will be focusing on the case of a UNIX workstation running Security Dynamics' sdshell program. That program is assigned to be the user's shell. Once the user has authenticated to /bin/login, they are passed to the sdshell, which communicates with the ACE/Server to obtain authentication information for the user. Although the attacks described here focus on the sdshell implementation, it is likely that they affect all implementations of the protocol. Version 1.2.4 of the sdshell is 49k. Later versions are reputed to have grown to as much as 80k for version 2.2. (All sparc binaries running on SunOS 4.1.4). There is also a client API which allows SecurIDs to be integrated into a new product on a supported platform without much involvement from Security Dynamics.

The server is comprised of a daemon, a database, and software to administer both. The server can be run on a variety of platforms, and has support for running over TCP/IP, Novell 3.11 and 3.12, and AppleTalk. Authentication can also be done via TACACS, XTACACS, and TACACS+. We focus on the TCP/IP implementation which is likely to be in use in most Internet connected networks. The protocol is stateless, and runs over UDP. The daemon listens on UDP port 124 by default. This has been changed in version 2. The database in version 1.2.4 was a proprietary flat database, and was replaced in version 2 by a Progress DBMS. The database and log files are stored DES encrypted, and can only be manipulated by the sdadmin program, or read by sdlogmon, respectively. The database stores information for each token: its planned death, the last successful login (in theory), the last attempt, the PIN, an estimate of the clock drift, and the card's seed. It also stores information about groups of users, and groups of machines, and which groups or users are allowed to login to each machine or group of machines. The system supports two servers, a master and a slave. We do not examine their interaction, and consider only the case of a single master, because the nature of the attack described here is not affected by the master-slave connection.

## II.     The Ace protocol

This paper examines the protocol as implemented in version 1.2.4 of the software. The purpose of the Ace protocol is to allow the token seed database and the card algorithm to remain on a single central machine which can then be well defended. The protocol, it is claimed, offers 'four successive levels of overlapping encryption' and 'mutually authenticates' the client and server (FAQ, 4.13). This claim of mutual authentication will be shown to be false.

The following terminology will be used through the textual and graphical (Figure 1) description of the protocol:

> **c** is a DES key previously generated by the client and sent to the server.
> $E_k$(**plaintext**) refers to the DES encryption of the plaintext with key K.
> **IP** is the IP address of the Ace client.[1]
> **P** is the passcode that the user would like to have authenticated.
> **p** is the passcode a particular token + pin is expected to produce
> **p+1, p-1** are the expected passcodes if the card's clock has drifted one quantum forward or back.
> **T** is a timestamp

**F2** is a hash developed by Security Dynamics. For the protocol to work as designed, it needs some secret input. F2 produces 256 bits of output from

---

[1] Note that the IP being tied to the host caused dual homing (more than one network card in a machine) to fail to work with Version 1 of the software, since machines were indexed by IP; no hostname was transmitted, and if two routes were available, the 'wrong' one might be chosen. This may also cause DHCP to fail, if the aceserver is conservatively configured to not use the DNS. If machine name were to be sent instead, then this would not be an issue.

its input. F2 can be derived from examining the "sdshell" program, which is available to the computer underground.

**WP** refers to a 'Workstation Passcode,' which is 64 bits of the 256 bits of output of F2. WP[1] refers to the first 64 bits.

The protocol begins when a user causes some server process (login, in.rshd, etc) to spawn their shell.

1. sdshell signals the server with a hello message (Figure 2).
2. aceserver responds with a timestamp, T (Figure 3).
3. sdshell prompts the user 'Enter Passcode:'
4. The user sends back the appropriate current passcode, P
5. sdshell calculates F2(IP, T, P), and splits it into wp[1-4]
6. sdshell sends a UDP packet with (username, $E_c$ (wp[1])).

(Figure 4)

7. aceserver decrypts the packet, and calculates F2(IP, T, p)

If the wp from that calculation matches what was sent by sdshell, then the assumption is made that the user has the card and pin, and should be allowed in. If not, aceserver calculates F2(IP, T, p+1) and F2(IP, T, p-1) and compares them to the value received.

8. If a match was successful, then an authorization message is sent to the sdshell: $E_{wp[2]}$(authorization), shell to run.

If a match is not found, aceserver looks for a match with p-10— p+10. It can send a message requesting a second tokencode, which allows it to ensure that its estimate of the card's clock drift is correct. It can also send back a failure message, encrypted with wp[1] as the key (FAQ 4.14).

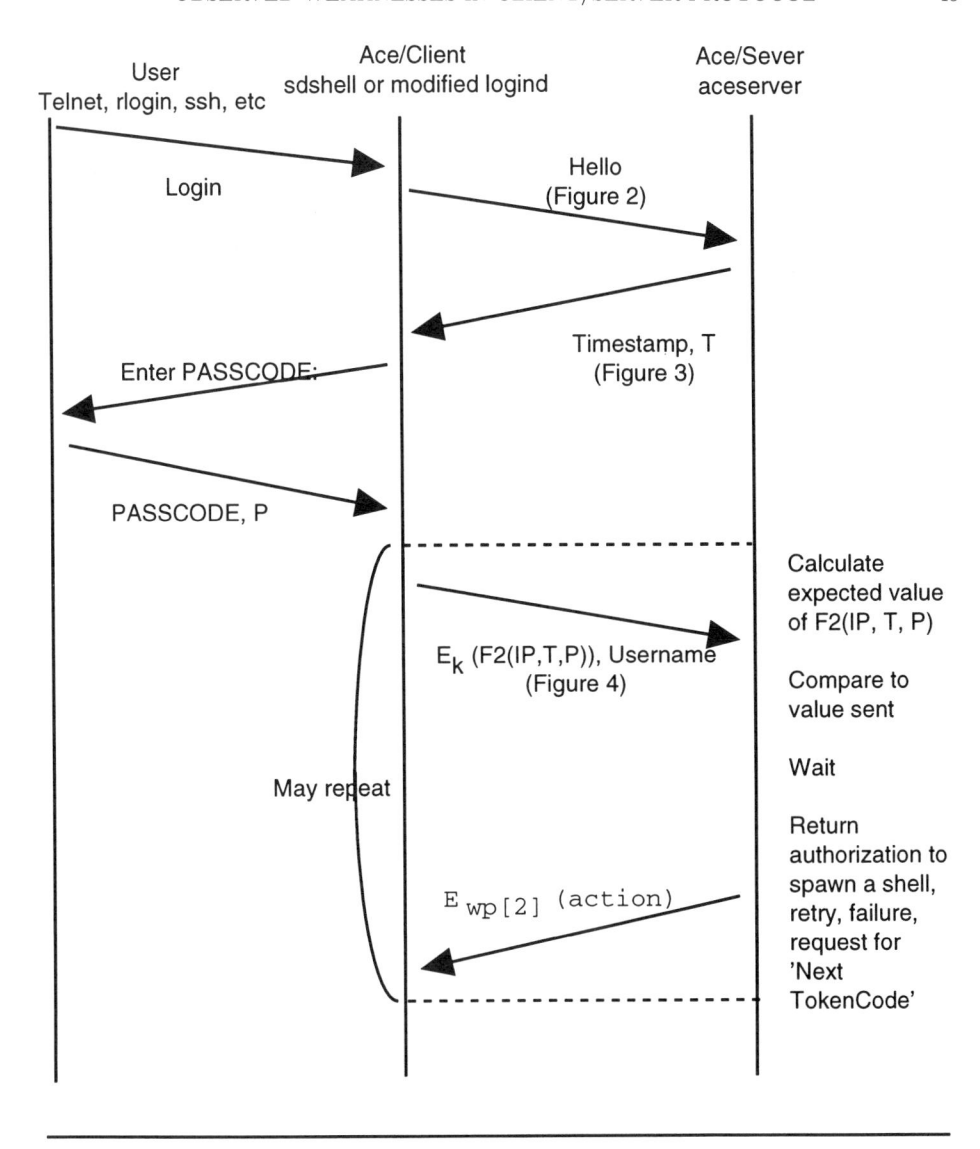

OBSERVED WEAKNESSES IN CLIENT/SERVER PROTOCOL

Figure 1. The Ace Client Server Protocol

The Packets:

These packet formats are not completely known at this time, but what we have found demonstrates some of the weak, non-cryptographic authentication taking place. Each packet is shown as the body of the udp packet, followed by an analysis of the packet. We do not show the authorization packet format.

Each packet contains several magic numbers and place holders, as well as some constants which are switched around according to set rules. There are also at least two sequence numbers in each packet.

Sequence A increments 1 for each packet client sends in a session.
Sequence B decrements 1 per packet
Sequence C increments by 5 each message
Sequence D decrements by 5 each message

A B C D and F are bytes that are sent back and forth with some transposition. E changes from session to session.
The username, unencrypted, is expressed in hex. (adam=61 64 61 6d)
Underlined bytes never seem to change within a packet type.

```
              8         16        24        32
       +----+----+----+----+----+----+----+----+
        4500 0098 1633 0000 3c11 517f cd88 41c6
        c034 4720 09a0 02f3 0084 0000 6702 0010
        0000 0000 0000 0000 0000 0000 0000 0000
       (208 more 0 bytes)

              8         16        24        32
       +----+----+----+----+----+----+----+----+
        Securid |SeqA|0000|mrkr|seqB| 'A'  'B'
        'C'  'D'|  'E'  'F' |0084 0000|6702 0010
```

Figure 2. (Hello)

```
              8            16           24           32
    +----+----+----+----+----+----+----+----+
    4500 0098 c9b2 0000 3111 a8ff c034 4720
    cd88 41c6 02f3 09a0 0084 0000 6c02 0010
    4a58 8000 0000 000a 3273 c5c6 003a 5bfa
    c92d 5cc2 b52d cdcd df39 0ce8 0cfa 0b54
    4b55 55dd 6bd9 e5fa 7931 7ee8 c72a 77a4
    3c16 d2f8 897b 5fc8 dcc4 0cc4 ae86 a1f4
    7279 e41d 66b3 100b a577 2c47 3762 d7d9
    ab50 36d8 56b3 55aa 0599 d30a 6be8 6191
    3349 3bff eafb 3a83 84e8 955e 4576 9071
    bc96 df03 07f4 7605

              8            16           24           32
    +----+----+----+----+----+----+----+----+
    Securid  |SeqC|0000|mrkr|seqD| 'C'  'D'
     'A'  'B'| 'F'  'E' |0084 0000|6702 0010
    4a58 8000 0000 000a 32| Encoded time
    roughly decodes to October 27 1996
    15.25 EST
```

Figure 3. Time

```
            8           16          24          32
+----+----+----+----+----+----+----+----+
4500 0098 1634 0000 3c11 517e cd88 41c6
c034 4720 09a0 02f3 0084 0000 6502 0010
0000 0000 6164 616d 0000 0000 0000 0000
0000 0000 0000 0000 0000 0000 0000 0000
0000 0000 0000 0000 0000 0000 0000 0000
0000 0000 0000 0000 0000 0000 0000 0000
0000 0000 0000 0001 2721 2e54 99da b278
561a 80cb a483 c1ee 0000 0000 0000 0000
0000 0000 0000 0000 0000 0000 0000 0000
0000 0000 0000 0000


+----+----+----+----+----+----+----+----+
 Securid   |SeqA|0000|mrkr|seqB|  'A'   'B'
  'C'  'D'|  'E'  'F' |0084 0000|6702 0010
 0000 0000|username   |0000 0000 0000 0000
 '0' characters to fill out to byte 201
 0000 0000 0000 0001| DES encrypted wp[1]
 DES (continued)    |0000 0000 0000 0000
```

Figure 4. Passcode verification request

## III. Attacking the Protocol

There appears to be essentially no private information in the key used in step 8. The key used, wp[2], is derived from three chunks of information: The IP address, the timestamp, and the passcode. The IP address is known to anyone who can connect to the machine to break in. The timestamp is slightly more difficult, but an Ace/Server will send it to any machine that can send it UDP packets. If you cannot get the timestamp, the time can be easily guessed, especially if the site is using NTP or some other time setting protocol which causes them to have accurate clocks. The passcode can be chosen by the attacker.

Thus, the key might have up to $2^6$ bits of information if time were granular to the second, but time appears to be granular to the minute. Since time packets are sent to anyone who requests them, the key has essentially no entropy.

1. Telnet to the target machine
2. Enter a sniffed username and password.
3. Send a time request to the Ace/Server

4. Compute wp[1] for F2(IP(target), T, 123456)
5. Find port sdshell will listen on
6. Send passcode of 123456
7. Package and send $DES_{wp[1]}$(Allow access) to sdshell on expected port
(See Figure 5)

The actual statefulness of the protocol is an open question. If there is substantial state in the protocol, and if it is checked, then the attack may only be practical if the attacker is on the local network already, because sniffing certain packets may be required to find the appropriate values.

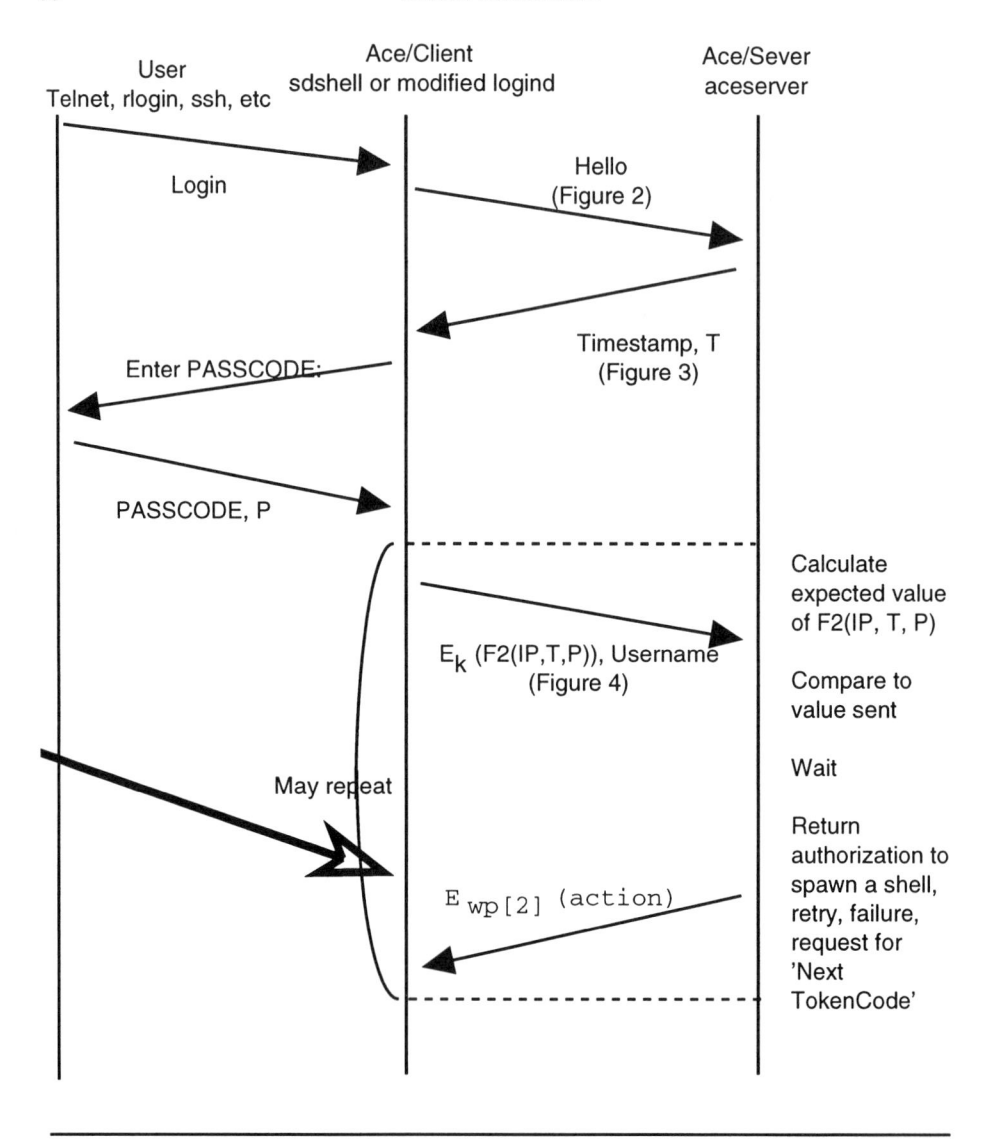

Figure 5, The Ace Client/Server Protocol Under Attack

Thus, any attacker with UDP access to the Ace/Client can send it a UDP packet that convinces sdshell that they are legitimate, and should be allowed in. (The attacker also needs the format of the authorization packet, the F2 hash, and a username and password.)

Timing the attack is quite easy. In response to a variety of sniff and race attacks, SDTI has added a delay in all authorization responses. The attacks being defended against involve watching legitimate users logging in, and mirroring their actions. At the very end of the login sequence, the attacker either sends in the "enter" character faster, or sends in all of the possible last digits to complete the authentication code. (These attacks have a roughly 30% chance of getting in, and are documented in (peiterz)). In response to these attacks, aceserver will delay from 1-15 seconds (administrator configurable) before responding to a request, and if it sees multiple requests in that time, will reject them all. However, this delay acts as a window of opportunity to forge the authorization packet. (It also opens an obvious denial of service attack.)

There is a practical difficulty in determining what port the sdshell will bind to. We expect that this port can be found fairly easily. If the last security offered by the protocol is in the difficulty of finding the port, then the system can fairly be termed security through obscurity. This is especially true if the attacker is local, and wants to impersonate another user. If the user is local, they need only to run the command "netstat -a" to find sdshell listening. If they are remote, an extended probe may be needed to find the port range to attack.

## IV.    Defending Your Site

The most obvious solution, of upgrading to a more recent version of the software is one obvious defense. We consider two groups of attackers, outsiders and insiders. The attacks by outsiders are easy to defeat, attacks by insiders are not.

To defend yourself against the attack being carried out from the outside, block all incoming udp packets, except those that you need, such as DNS. This is a good policy anyway, and many sites that already do this will not need to take any action, except to verify that things work as designed.

Defending against insiders is not so easy. You lose the ability to use SecurID if you block udp packets. We urge those sites who use SecurID for internal authentication to require Security Dynamics to provide protocol fixes that have been subjected to peer review. Fixing this problem will require an update for each sdshell deployed. Installing anti-sniffing hubs, or deploying IPsecurity may provide sufficient defenses. However, none of these can be done quickly or cheaply. Note that session encryption provides no defense, since this is an attack on the authorization mechanism for a user's session, not one that involves stealing passcodes. Also, it is worth considering using a different authentication tool for your Ace/Server until you are confident this problem has been fixed.

Insiders who want to masquerade as a different user on their local host have a particularly easy time of it, with access to the port numbers, time stamp, and other information.

## V.     Fixing the protocol

The protocol should be stateful. A stateful protocol would allow this problem to be fixed with a small change to the server software, namely, replacing the timestamp sent out with a nonce of the same size. That would put enough information out of the reach of the attacker to make the attack impractical. It would also allow for easy detection when one user is trying to login multiple times on the same machine. In addition, a stateful protocol would require enough network access to forge TCP sequence numbers, which is more work than is needed in the case of a UDP based protocol.

The key used in the final step should be the previously negotiated secret key. That will fix the problem, by making it difficult to send a forged packet that will be accepted as authentic by sdshell but require updates to all the software deployed. Changing key management procedures is of course fraught with risk. That risk is probably less than continuing with the problems shown herein, and can be mitigated by proper cryptographic design. Confidence in the new protocol can be enhanced by publishing the protocols, and subjecting them to peer review.

It may seem sensible to separate the authentication and encryption keys. The possibility of signing the final authentication message should be considered. However, using a separate key that needs to be shared with each machine puts a large burden on the server to manage keys, where one DES key will do as well as two or more. The keys should probably be changed automatically from time to time to protect against an attacker who has obtained root access to the machine continuing to be able to get in, by his knowledge of the cryptographic keys.[2]

## VI.    Future Directions

### A.    For Research

---

[2]There are few systems which do well once the attacker has compromised the keys. Thus attacks against the system when session keys are known to an attacker are not examined in detail.

The random numbers used as the client DES key seem to be generated fairly quickly, and may be weak. This observation is from personal experimentation with forced key regeneration. The process is much faster than generating SKIP, PGP, or other long lived keys. There may be order of magnitude improvements available over a brute force search of the DES key space. Obtaining known plaintext for these attacks is easy; depending on the strength of F2, obtaining chosen plaintext may also be feasible.

Version 2.1 and 2.2 of the software use an X11 based GUI, and require that at least some portion of the X libraries be installed. There are probably exploitable weaknesses in most configurations that would enable an attacker to breach the security of the Ace/Server. Those worried about this should probably isolate the Ace/Server, and only administrate it locally, or via SSH, or some other encryption package that ensures the X components will not weaken the system as a whole.

B.  For Security Dynamics

Publishing a protocol before it is widely deployed may prevent this sort of problem in the future. Even the best people miss things, and putting the protocol out for public review assures that the good guys as well as the bad can be assured of its strength.

There have been persistent rumors that SecurID was trivially bypassed for a long time. This may be the result of this, or other, problems[3]. As long as the protocol is hidden, it takes a lot of effort to find problems. For a long time, only the bad guys have had sufficient amounts of time and motivation.

## VII. Contacts with Security Dynamics

Security Dynamics was first notified of this bug in July 1996, when Mark Warner and Chris MacNeil told us that the bug had been found and fixed by adding the client secret key into the information hashed by F2, thus, wp=F2(IP, T, P, c). Details about when this happened were not provided. When we asked John Brainard about this in August, he suggested that the attack would work. Security Dynamics was notified about the planned publication of this paper in November.

When a draft was provided, Security Dynamics responded with several minor corrections to the paper, and the knowledge that this would not work with their current products and protocols. I have endeavored to correct the minor errors where they occured.

## VIII. Acknowledgments

---

[3]TCP hijacking is a strong possibility.

Andrew Gross, Mark Chen, Bruce Schneier, and Matt Blaze provided advice, encouragement and guidance. Marcus Ranum and Shabbir Safdar provided useful feedback on drafts.

## IX. References

[Brainard] John Brainard, private communication
[FAQ] Security Dynamics, *Securid FAQ*,
http://www.securid.com/ID51.162015188143/Resources/FAQs/sdfaq3.html
http://www.securid.com/ID51.162015188143/Resources/FAQs/sdfaq4.html
[peiterz] peiterz, *Weaknesses In SecurID*
[Schneier] Bruce Schneier, *Applied Cryptography: Protocols, Algorithms, and Source Code in C, Second Ed.* John Wiley and Sons, New York, 1996.

The author is an independent consultant specializing in information security issues.

*E-mail:* adam@homeport.org

# Web Security: A High Level View
## *Extended Abstract*

### Drew Dean

The explosive growth of the Internet has brought about a corresponding growth in security problems. While the IP protocol[7] has a provision for a security label in each datagram, this option has received little use. The meaning of the labels is only useful to the national security community, and no mechanism for tamper-proofing them is provided. In this abstract, we examine the HTTP protocol underlying the World Wide Web, discuss threats, and some of their solutions.

The HTTP/1.0 protocol[2] is remarkably simple. Each transaction opens a new TCP connection. There are 3 commands: `GET`, `POST`, and `HEAD`. (Four other commands are defined in an appendix, but have not seen much use.) `GET` retrieves a URL, and `POST` sends the information (presumably from a form), and reads the result. `HEAD` returns meta-information about a given URL. Meta-information is encoded in MIME headers, e.g., `Content-Type:`, `Content-Length:`, etc. This is about as simple as things can be. So what can go wrong? Plenty. The first set of attacks to consider are spoofing attacks. There are many things that can be spoofed: DNS and IP addresses are the two most obvious. Executable content enables new content spoofing attacks[5]. The good news is that we almost know how to prevent spoofing: the proper application of cryptographic techniques (cryptography, digital signatures, etc.) will solve the problem. Note the words "almost" and "proper" — these are critical. Peter Neumann's work has shown that securely embedding cryptography into a system is a non-trivial job[6]. Web spoofing also works against "secure" connections over SSL, because cryptography can only ensure that the browser has connected to the machine named in the URL, but that may be a different machine than the one the human user thinks that they are connected to.

Let us now look at client-side security, i.e., what the user running Netscape Navigator, Microsoft Internet Explorer, or a similar user agent, needs to be concerned about. Ignoring executable content for the moment, the security requirement would seem to be quite simple: they merely display a document written in plain ASCII or HTML, a well documented standard[3]. The images are also in well-known formats. Alas, it is not quite so simple. All of the common web browsers are written in unsafe programming languages, where the language provides no support for detecting buffer overflows, running off the end of an array, etc. It is a folk theorem that any crash due to an erroneous memory write (e.g., writing via a "smashed" pointer) is a potential security flaw. The question is: "How difficult is it for the attacker to control the value of the erroneous pointer?" It may be quite hard (and

---

1991 *Mathematics Subject Classification*. Primary 68-02.
This work was supported in part by a fellowship from Bellcore.

effectively unexploitable), or it may be quite simple (e.g., in case of a buffer overflow). Unfortunately, the current crop of web browsers seem to crash at least moderately often. It is unknown how many of these crashes are due to erroneous writes, but undoubtably some of them are. (Some others are due to erroneous reads, which may also be possible to exploit.) While these attacks may be difficult to exploit, they are clearly a threat for mission-critical systems (i.e., information warfare). These attacks pose a larger threat in the future: electronic commerce will mean that your computer can spend money. Illicit monetary gain has motivated much more sophisticated attacks than these throughout history, and there is no reason to believe that this will change.

If a web browser finds a `Content-Type:` it does not know how to handle, it will give the content to another (user-specified) "helper" program that knows how to interpret the data. Unfortunately, many of these programs were not written with security in mind. (That is, they never expected to be receiving untrusted input.) Bugs in these applications can lead to system penetration. Newer browsers also support "plug-ins" which are dynamically loaded into the browser, and execute in the same process as the browser. While one might hope that more attention is paid to security during their development, because the developers know that they will be receiving untrusted input, plug-ins pose an even larger architectural challenge, because the underlying operating system has no way to differentiate them from the user's browser.

Executable content makes client-side security infinitely more complicated. We now have to consider the effects of an untrusted program running on the system. As pointed out by Steve Bellovin, this breaks an implicit assumption in most firewalls: that all the "bad guys" are on the outside. Confining executable content to a safe arena, while allowing for interesting applications is an open problem. Significant problems have been found in Java[4] and JavaScript. The all-or-nothing trust model of ActiveX may be good for large software vendors, but it offers the user little guidance whether they should trust software written by "Flight By Night Software, Inc." Alas, the joy of the web is that everyone can publish information on an equal footing: ActiveX does not effectively support this model.

Moving over to the web server, we again find a seemingly simple program that turns out to be rather complicated in reality. Nominally, a HTTP server receives a request (in the form of a URL and other information encoded in MIME headers), and sends back some document (e.g., a HTML file, a text file, etc.). This is fairly simple, although the same sorts of bugs discussed above (buffer overflow, etc.) can happen here, with equally bad consequences. The complication comes in the Common Gateway Interface (CGI) support found in modern web servers, along with server-side executable content.

The CGI architecture allows the author of a web page to specify that a program will be run to generate the contents of a URL. While this is quite powerful (almost all forms feed their data back to a CGI program), it is also extremely dangerous. Examine the security situation here carefully: Assume that the web server is run with the permissions of some system user (possibly, but not necessarily the superuser, but somewhat more privileged than an ordinary user). We now have the server executing a program written by a user who is semi-trusted at best, receiving input from a completely untrusted source. The external source could be attempting to penetrate the system, or the user could be attempting to gain additional privileges, or both. (Note that this situation is isomorphic to a mail transfer agent that will deliver mail to a program specified by the user.[1] The history of `sendmail`[1] is not particularly encouraging.) Present mass-market operating systems do not have useful confinement abilities for preventing either kind of abuse.

---

[1] This was originally pointed out by Edward Felten.

JavaSoft is developing a web server as part of their Java Server project that will run client-specified Java bytecode "servlets." This seems inherently risky: a servlet's access to the web server cannot be quite as limited as what a Java applet receives in a web browser; if servlets cannot query databases, they will not be very useful. At the same time, the set of queries a servlet can make needs to be restricted; the classic problems of database inference and aggregation rear their heads.

A rather bleak picture has been painted so far. What can be done about these problems? Executable content seems particularly difficult to support with present systems. A strong way to provide a strict subset of the user's privileges is required. This can either be implemented in the operating system, or in the executable content's runtime system (the approach Java attempts). The second approach has not been successful so far, but still has promise. A small, formally defined language, with proven type-soundness, should provide an interesting base to build a system on. We need to understand the mapping between the source language and what is actually sent to be executed at a remote site. Java was not designed to meet these criteria.

As to the implementation of web servers and user agents, this is a classic software engineering problem: we are really asking how to build reliable software. Safe languages, while not a panacea, relieve the programmer of many painful details that must be gotten correct. Formal methods have a place, too, in proving important theorems about high-level design issues, although formally proven implementations are not presently feasible. The payoff from formal methods is not just the proof; it is the bugs found that prevented the original proof attempt from going through. Unfortunately, the mass market is not yet interested in secure software; it is more interested in which browser has the most features and ships first. It seems that it will require a widely publicized, very expensive problem to change this attitude.

The original security situation in the web was conceptually simple: everything was static. While proper implementation was difficult, primarily due to the implementation technology used, the model was simple. Various executable content systems, along with CGI programs and servlets, have evolved both the client and server into complicated security situations, with insufficient support from the underlying programming languages and operating systems. Electronic commerce will motivate sophisticated attacks. Cryptography does not address these issues; however, it appears to offer a solution to the spoofing problems, if properly deployed. Web security promises to be an active area for many years to come.

## References

[1] Allman, Eric, "SENDMAIL — An Internetwork Mail Router," Chapter 9 in *4.4BSD System Manager's Manual*, O'Reilly and Associates, Inc., April, 1994.
[2] Berners-Lee, Tim, et al., "Hypertext Transfer Protocol," RFC 1945, 1996.
[3] Berners-Lee, Tim, et al., "Hypertext Markup Language - 2.0," RFC 1866, November 1995.
[4] Dean, D., E. Felten, and D. Wallach, "Java Security: From HotJava to Netscape and Beyond," *Proceedings of the 1996 IEEE Symposium on Security and Privacy*, Oakland, CA, May 1996.
[5] Felten, E., D. Balfanz, D. Dean, and D. Wallach, "Web Spoofing: An Internet Con Game," Technical Report 540-96, Department of Computer Science, Princeton University, December 1996.
[6] Neumann, Peter, "Can Systems Be Trustworthy with Software-Implemented Cryptography?" Technical Report, Computer Science Laboratory, SRI International, Menlo Park, CA, October 1994.
[7] Postel, Jon, "Internet Protocol," RFC 791, 1981.

DEPARTMENT OF COMPUTER SCIENCE, PRINCETON UNIVERSITY, 35 OLDEN ST., PRINCETON, NJ 08544

*E-mail address*: ddean@cs.princeton.edu

# Flexible, Extensible Java Security Using Digital Signatures

Dan S. Wallach
dwallach@cs.princeton.edu

Jim A. Roskind
jar@netscape.com

Edward W. Felten
felten@cs.princeton.edu

ABSTRACT. Java's original "sandbox" model for security enforced the same security policy for all applets, regardless of origin or trust. As a result, the security policy had to be necessarily restrictive to prevent untrusted applets from damaging the user's machine. We describe a system for associating cryptographic digital signature principals with Java classes, and managing which privileges are associated with those principals. This system addresses the needs of application writers for less restrictive security policies, and mediates trust among mutually suspicious objects in the Java system, and will be shipping as part of Netscape Navigator 4.0.

## 1. Introduction

Java, and the notion of secure execution of untrusted code from across the network, has gained much attention since its introduction. Java programs are distributed as bytecode and run in users' web browsers, generally in the same address space as the browser, but with fewer privileges than the user running the browser. Java restricts malicious programs by restricting dangerous primitives (i.e., access to the network or local file-system), and by enforcing type-safety (i.e., preventing forged pointers or illegal invocation of private methods) [1]. This is usually called the sandbox model, and all Java applets are restricted to this same security policy.

In Internet Explorer 3.0, Microsoft introduced Authenticode [2], which digitally signs native machine code or Java bytecode and allows the user to either grant the code full access to all machine resources, or to completely block its execution. Once executing, such code can maliciously (or accidentally) crash or damage the system. This is usually called the shrink-wrap model, as it parallels the physical purchase and installation of software from a computer store. We set out to design a system that takes advantage of digital signatures to make Java security more flexible, without settling for the all-or-nothing choice presented by the shrink-wrap model.

## 2. Main ideas

This section presents the main ideas of our design. Our presentation will reason from our requirements to the features of our system, so that our design choices will be clear. Our goal in this section is not to describe all of the details — that will come later — but to provide an outline of our system.

---

1991 *Mathematics Subject Classification.* Primary 68N25.

Dan Wallach did portions of this work at Netscape Communications Corp., and is supported by a fellowship from Bellcore. Edward W. Felten is supported in part by an NSF National Young Investigator award.

Our design must meet three fundamental requirements. First, it must provide the flexibility necessary to address the needs of users, site administrators, and authors of applets and utilities: to allow some code to have more privileges than Java's sandbox model allows, to support trusted applets and trusted subsystems, to avoid imposing too many choices on the user, and to allow site administrators to impose mandatory security policies.

Second, our design must satisfy the *principle of least privilege* [3]: we should try to minimize the trust placed in principals and pieces of code. (We note that the current JDK (Java Development Kit) 1.0 runtime system violates this principle by treating the entire Java runtime library as completely trusted.)

Third, we are not allowed to modify the Java language or the interfaces provided by the Java runtime library; nor are we allowed to make very large modifications to the Java virtual machine. We are limited to the addition of new library functions and small virtual machine modifications.

### 2.1. Principal privileges.
A running Java system contains code from many sources and with many authors. There may be several applets running, and the Java runtime library itself is large and should be decomposed into pieces with different levels of trust.

To manage these different sources of code, we must label each piece of code with its source. Specifically, we will label each Java class with a list of *principals* under whose authority the class is running. Principals will digitally sign code that they endorse, and the system will deduce the endorsement from the signature.

Decisions about how much to trust a piece of code will be based on a security policy. The policy may come from several sources: the user, a site administrator, or the Java runtime library, itself. Each of these players may state a security policy; we combine the policies into a single overall policy by using the *consensus-voting rule* (see section 3.2): forbid the action if any of the players votes to forbid it; otherwise allow it if any of the players votes to allow it; if no player votes either way, forbid the action.

Since a signature on code implies endorsement of that code, we will sometimes have code signed by more than one principal. Again, we need a way to combine the policies with respect to the individual principals into a single overall policy. Again, we use the consensus voting rule.

These mechanisms allow us to assign *class privileges* to every piece of code, saying which actions that code has authority to request.

### 2.2. Scope privileges.
When the time comes to determine whether a requested action should be allowed, we want to ask two questions:

- On whose authority is the request being made?
- Does that principal have privileges to authorize the requested action?

Principal privileges speak only to the second question. We need an additional mechanism to address the first question.

Since we could not modify the interface to the Java runtime library, we could not add additional arguments to the library calls to carry this information. Therefore we need to infer the information from the environment in which the request is made. We call the inferred information *scope privileges*, because it depends on the dynamic scope in which the request is being made.

A tempting but inadequate approach to scope privileges is to say that if, for example, the `net_connect()` call is being made to open a network connection, then the request is being made under the authority of the principal whose code directly called

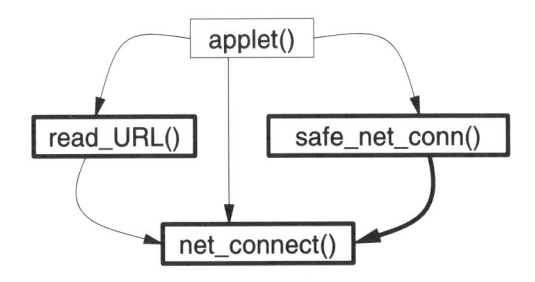

FIGURE 1. There are several ways for an applet to cause net_connect() to be invoked. Decisions about whether to allow the network connection depend on the exact call-path followed. Bold boxes indicate trusted classes and bold arrows indicate calls with privileges enabled.

net_connect(). This handles the case, shown in figure 1, in which an applet calls directly into net_connect(). The action is requested with the applet's authority.

Figure 1 also illustrates why this approach fails. The problem is that an applet may have called the library routine read_URL() which then called net_connect(). Clearly, read_URL() was called with the authority of the applet; read_URL() would like to be able to call net_connect() with the authority of the applet, such that normal security checks may occur. However, in this case net_connect() would be called with the authority of the runtime library, creating a security hole. This implies that we need to base authorization decisions on more than just the identity of the procedure that is requesting the operation.

On the other hand, figure 1 also shows the safe_net_connect() procedure, which checks to make sure the applet wants to connect to an approved host, and if so asserts its own authority to call net_connect(). We need a way to distinguish procedures like safe_net_connect(), which want to assert their own authority, from procedures like read_URL(), which want to use the authority of their caller.

This is not an unrealistic example — there are many cases like it in the Java runtime libraries. The solution is to base the authorization decision not only on the authority of the direct caller of a procedure, but also on the authority of indirect callers: on procedures higher up the call-stack. Indeed, this is how the current JDK 1.0 SecurityManager works.

The current JDK 1.0 SecurityManager design suffers from an important flaw: it requires the decision-maker to look up the stack and make its decision based only on the identities of the direct and indirect callers. The problem is that knowing that a principal's code is on the call-stack is different from knowing that that principal has authorized an action. The decision-making code must infer, from the sequence of procedures on the call-stack, whose authority is being asserted. This seems unduly error-prone; what we want is a way for a procedure to explicitly say that it is using its authority.

This leads to our definition of *scope privileges*. We allow a procedure to call enablePrivilege() to explicitly use its right to authorize a particular action. This operation succeeds if the caller has principal privileges for that action; thus a procedure's scope privileges are always a subset of its principal privileges. The scope privileges persist until they are explicitly disabled, or until the procedure returns, whichever comes first.

We also provide a rule for automatic passing of scope privileges from caller to callee. If A calls B, then the scope privileges of B are initially set equal to the *intersection* of A's scope privileges and B's principal privileges. In other words, the callee receives those scope privileges which (a) the caller had enabled and (b) the callee could have gained for itself anyway.

This privilege propagation rule is a very important part of our design. The alternative, to blindly pass on *all* of the caller's scope privileges to the callee, would allow attacks in which untrusted code acquired illegitimate privileges by luring trusted code into calling it. This is a serious concern, since there are many cases in the Java runtime system in which system threads call back into user-provided classes; for example, this is common in the graphical user interface code.

Later in the paper we will describe our design more formally, and demonstrate its flexibility by showing several examples of its use.

**2.3. Problems not solved.** When designing this system, there were a number of problems we deliberately chose *not* to solve. We did not specify any particular digital signature format, nor did we specify how signatures are associated with Java classes. Instead, we make fairly modest demands on signatures — they only indicate a *principal* for a given class. Signatures say nothing about what privileges a class may be granted. Thus, any signature standard suitable for electronic mail (to validate the origin of a mail message) should be suitable for this system.

We did not attempt to assign privileges to *specific* programs or applets. All privileges are associated strictly with principals. As a program is upgraded and patched, it's difficult to say what remains constant, except its cryptographic principals. While URLs (or other forms of network addresses) could potentially be used to identify specific applets, they do not provide strong guarantees against tampering.

We also chose to rely on the integrity of Java's type system [4]. While this may not necessarily be a safe assumption [5], an attacker who can break the type system can execute arbitrary machine code and circumvent any security mechanism we might create. Without assuming an impractical level of support from the operating system to create memory-protection boundaries, the Java type-system is the only suitable protection mechanism available. As hardware vendors aggressively identify and repair bugs in their systems, Java vendors have been aggressive at fixing Java type-system bugs and we ultimately rely on this.

Finally, we are not directly addressing non-interference [6] or covert channels among Java applets or with external systems such as firewalls or the Domain Name System (DNS). The focus of our system is to mediate access to previously unavailable primitives, rather than to significantly increase the assurance of the Java runtime.

## 3. System design

Our security infrastructure can be decomposed into a number of different sections. First, digital signatures may be applied to Java classes, associating these classes with principals. Then, a policy engine makes decisions about *who* is allowed to do *what*, possibly consulting the user. Finally, a run-time mechanism allows code to operate with less than its full privileges, limiting its exposure to external attacks.

**3.1. Digital signatures.** A digital signature on a Java class (the unit in which Java code is transported) represents an endorsement of the code by the signer: the signer is asserting that the code is not malicious and behaves as advertised. Since different people

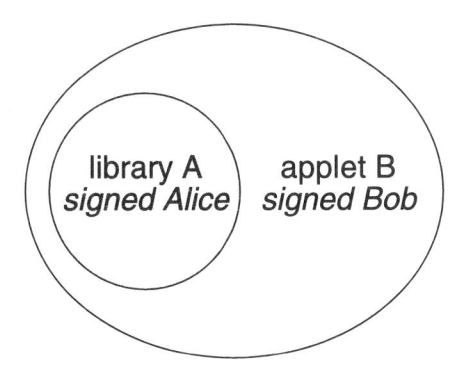

FIGURE 2. Alice's library, signed by Alice, ships in Bob's applet. Bob signs the entire applet, including Alice's library. Alice's library may operate with higher privileges than Bob's code.

trust the endorsements of different signers, we expect it will be common for classes to carry more than one signature. These digital signatures are abstracted to *principals*, which are the basis of security policies. Principals map one-to-one with private keys.

In addition to defining principals, signatures can allow one class to guarantee that its helper classes have not been corrupted in transit. In many respects, this property is taken for granted when a normal program's object files are linked into a binary image, and one signature is applied to the final program. While an active attacker could delete the signature and then change any class, the classes, in the absence of their signature, would also lack their privileges.

Since multiple principals may sign different *subsets* of the classes, we can implement a form of trusted subsystems (see figure 2). *Alice* creates a trusted library, signs it, and *Bob* includes it in his applet. Both Alice and Bob want to guarantee that when they reference a class which has not yet been loaded, the class which is loaded corresponds to the class they intended. If Bob wishes to abuse Alice's privileges, he must either call legal methods on her classes, which she protects, or he must modify her bytecode, violating her signature. If Bob removes Alice's signature entirely, her privileges will not be available, either.

**3.2. Permissions.** Access to system resources may be granted or blocked by separate parts of the system. For example, a user may give permission for some resources and an administrator may block others. We need a consistent algebra for reconciling the policy judgements of these subsystems. A *permission* may have one of three values: *allowed*, *forbidden*, or *abstain*. Colloquially, these correspond to granting permission, denying permission, or abstaining from the decision. The algebra corresponds to a consensus government: all non-abstaining votes, of which there must be at least one, must be in favor of an action for it to be permitted. Permission combination is commutative and associative.

$$(1) \quad \begin{matrix} \text{allowed} \\ \text{allowed} \\ \text{abstain} \\ \text{allowed} \\ \text{abstain} \\ \text{forbidden} \end{matrix} + \begin{matrix} \text{allowed} \\ \text{abstain} \\ \text{abstain} \\ \text{forbidden} \\ \text{forbidden} \\ \text{forbidden} \end{matrix} = \begin{matrix} \text{allowed} \\ \text{allowed} \\ \text{abstain} \\ \text{forbidden} \\ \text{forbidden} \\ \text{forbidden} \end{matrix}$$

Also note that

$$\begin{aligned}\forall x, \text{forbidden} + x &= \text{forbidden}\\ \forall x, \text{abstain} + x &= x\end{aligned} \quad (2)$$

**3.3. Targets.** A target[1] represents a resource or set of resources that somebody wants to protect. A target may refer to a machine resource, such as a microphone device, or it may refer to a sensitive piece of data.

Targets are named with a (*prin*, *name*) pair, where *prin* is a principal of the code which created the target and *name* is a character string (e.g., "unrestricted-file-read" or "unrestricted-network"). Any piece of Java code may create a target, provided the code was signed by the principal whose name appears in the target. Initially, the only targets are those defined by the *System* principal; these represent objects that the Java system itself wants to protect, such as filesystem access, network access, etc.

We also support *macro targets*, which are sets of other targets. In an effort to simplify a user's experience with the system, macro targets such as "typical game privileges" and "personal search engine privileges" are provided. These macro targets will be easier for the user to understand than a set of targets such as "access to the sound device, the graphics device, the microphone, and file access to a specific subdirectory." Anyone may create a macro target, but all the targets that make up the macro must have the same principal as the macro. This helps prevent spoofing attacks, which might fool a user into granting privileges for dangerous targets, hidden in a macro with an innocuous-sounding name. Macro targets exist only for convenience. With the exception of the user interface, the security code deals only with primitive targets; when a macro target is passed into the security code, the macro target is effectively "expanded" into its component primitive targets.

Finally, some targets, such as those for the filesystem and network, may wish to allow a subset of all possible files or network connections. These *parameterized targets* grant principals permission conditionally; the target is passed the arguments to the actual resource (e.g., file names or network addresses) and may impose more fine-grained security policies.

**3.4. Runtime enforcement model.** We now describe our security model more precisely. The model specifies the semantics that the implementation must satisfy, but it does not determine the implementation strategy. In particular, though the model is explained in terms of eager evaluation — computing the exact set of privileges at every point in time — the current implementation is lazy, computing privilege information only when needed. Since the implementation makes the same decision as the model, lazy evaluation does not affect the semantics; the purposes of using lazy evaluation are to ease implementation and to improve performance.

3.4.1. *Policies.* The model protects the access of *principals* to *targets*. A *policy* is a function which, given a (principal, target) pair, returns a permission: *allowed, abstain,* or *forbidden*. The user may define a policy, denoted $P_u$, and the site administrator may define a policy, denoted $P_s$. Informally, these policies capture the security desires of the user and the site administrator.

Each target $\tau$ defines its own policy $P_\tau$, subject to the rule that a target's security policy must answer *abstain* to all questions except those relating to the target itself. Formally, for all values of *prin* and *target*, either $P_\tau(\textit{prin, target}) = \textit{abstain}$ or $\tau = \textit{target}$.

---

[1] *Principal* and *target*, as used in this paper, are the same as *subject* and *object*, as used in the security literature, but are more clear for discussing security in object-oriented systems.

(3) $$\forall prin, \forall target, Policy(prin, target) = P_u(prin, target) + P_s(prin, target) + \sum_{\tau \in Targets} P_\tau(prin, target)$$

(4) $$\forall class, \forall target, ClassPolicy(class, target) = \begin{cases} abstain & \text{if } prin(class) = \emptyset \\ \sum_{p \in prin(class)} Policy(p, target) & \text{otherwise} \end{cases}$$

(5) $$\forall class, ClassPrivileges(class) = \{\tau \mid ClassPolicy(class, \tau) = allowed\}.$$

FIGURE 3. Equations defining the formal version of the model.

We can now derive the *overall policy*, written *Policy(.,.)*, by combining all of the policies defined so far, using the consensus-voting rule. The formal definition is given in equation 4; note that addition denotes the consensus-voting rule.

3.4.2. *The Class Policy.* Now that we know the policy for each principal, we can compute a policy for each Java class. Recall that a class might be signed by multiple principals; we define *prin(C)* to be the set of principals that have signed class *C*. We want to combine the policies for all of these principals using the consensus-voting rule. The formal definition of *ClassPolicy* is given in equation 5; again, addition denotes the consensus-voting rule.

3.4.3. *Class Privileges.* Now that we have a policy for each class, we can compute for each class its *class privileges*: the set of targets for which it is *allowed*. The formal definition of *ClassPrivileges* is given in equation 6.

3.4.4. *Scope privileges.* The final step is to give a formal definition of scope privileges. Intuitively, the scope privileges of a method invocation say which targets that invocation is allowed to operate on.

Our model adds an implicit argument, which we call scopePrivileges, to every Java method. scopePrivileges defines the set of targets that the method is allowed to access. The scopePrivileges argument is not explicitly passed by the Java code: it is handled automatically by the Java virtual machine (with our extensions). The scopePrivileges argument cannot be accessed or modified by ordinary Java code, except via the operators defined below. Since scopePrivileges is an argument to the method, its value pertains only to one particular invocation of the method, and the value "evaporates" when the method returns.

When a new Java thread is created, the thread starts its life by invoking some method. This invocation has its scopePrivileges set to the empty set.

When one method calls another, the callee's scopePrivileges is passed the intersection of the caller's scopePrivileges and *ClassPrivileges(calleeClass)*. Intuitively, the caller's privileges are passed on to the callee, subject to the constraint that the callee may not receive any privilege which it could not obtain for itself through other means.

In addition to the automatic propagation of scope privileges defined above, Java code may perform two explicit operations to modify scope privileges. The operation

| Principal | | Scope Privilege Operations |
|---|---|---|
| user | user1() | |
| user | user2() | |
| user | user3() | |
| System | safe_net_conn() | +networking |
| System | net_connect() | |
| System | checkPrivilege() | |

FIGURE 4. `safe_net_connect()` enables *networking* privileges before calling the low-level `net_connect()` Grey areas indicate enabled scope privileges for *networking*.

`enablePrivilege(s)`, where s is a set of targets, is equivalent to the following Java code[2]:

```
scopePrivileges = scopePrivileges ∪
    (s ∩ ClassPrivileges(thisClass));
```

The operation `disablePrivilege(s)`, where s is a set of targets, is equivalent to the following Java code:

```
scopePrivileges = scopePrivileges - s;
```

Informally, `enablePrivilege()` "turns on" some privileges that the current class is allowed to assert, and `disablePrivilege()` "turns off" some privileges.

The operation `checkPrivilege(s)`, where s is a set of targets, evaluates to true iff $s \subseteq$ scopePrivileges. Informally, `checkPrivilege()` checks whether the current scope is allowed to access some set of targets.

The model provides the operators defined above. It is up to the Java runtime libraries and applet code to use these operators to protect their sensitive data and methods. Below we give several examples of how this is done.

**3.5. Examples.** To understand the system in detail, let us consider a series of examples concerning access control of the network.

3.5.1. *Default policy.* The default Java policy is to allow network connections to be created only to the host from which the applet originated. Here, we show how this policy could be re-implemented in our framework. We first define a target called (*System, networking*)[3]. The network-related code in the Java runtime library is signed by the *System* principal, and the policy will *allow* access to *networking* by *System*.

The `safe_net_connect()` procedure executes `enablePrivilege(networking)` if the requested connection is to the host of the applet's origin; otherwise `safe_net_connect()` does not manipulate the scope privileges at all (see figure 4). When `safe_net_connect()` calls the low-level `net_connect()` procedure, `net_connect()` will proceed with the connection iff `checkPrivilege(networking)` succeeds.

---

[2]For clarity, we assume here that Java has a *set* datatype, and supports intersection, union, and set-difference operators on sets.

[3]Referred to as "*networking*" elsewhere for simplicity

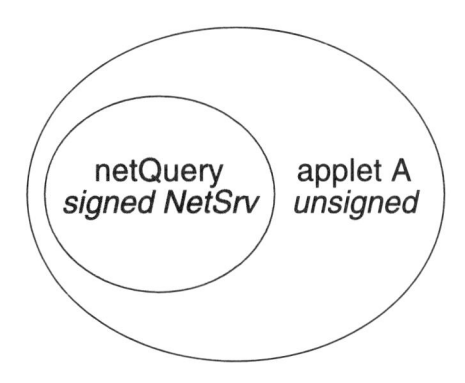

FLEXIBLE, EXTENSIBLE JAVA SECURITY USING DIGITAL SIGNATURES  67

FIGURE 5. NetSrv provides a subsystem, trusted to connect to their server, usable by any applet.

| Principal | | Scope Privilege Operations |
|---|---|---|
| | A1() | |
| | A2() | |
| NetSrv | Netsrv1() | +networking |
| NetSrv | Netsrv2() | |
| System | read_URL() | |
| System | net_connect() | |
| System | checkPrivilege() | |

FIGURE 6. NetSrv enables *networking* privileges before calling the system code. Grey areas indicate enabled scope privileges.

Note that the applet cannot violate security by directly calling `net_connect()`. The connection is allowed only if the scope privileges for the *networking* target are enabled, and the only way to do this is to call through `safe_net_connect()`.

3.5.2. *Trusted applet.* Suppose a user wanted to designate some principal as authorized to connect to any network address. The user will change his policy to *allow* the *networking* target for that principal. Code signed by that principal could then amplify its privileges to include *networking* and call directly into `net_connect()`.

3.5.3. *Trusted subsystem.* Rather than trust an unknown vendor, users are more likely to trust name-brands. Such a trusted vendor can create and digitally sign a set of Java classes that implements a trusted subsystem. These classes, distributed with any applet, can extend the security model in a controlled way. For example, a subsystem may allow the applet to connect to a specific host on the network other than the host where the applet originated. An example is shown in figure 5, in which the trusted subsystem allows a connection to the *NetSrv* stock-market-data service to which the user has subscribed. To make this work, it is imperative that the extended privileges are only available to the trusted classes, and not to all classes in the system.

In our example, the policy is changed to *allowed* access to the *networking* target by principal *NetSrv*. The trusted `NetSrv1()` method calls `enablePrivilege`(*networking*), as shown in figure 6 and then eventually calls `net_connect()` to connect to the appropriate machine at NetSrv headquarters.

| Principal | | Scope Privilege Operations |
|---|---|---|
| System | sys1() | |
| System | sys2() | +networking |
| System | sys3() | |
| user | user_callback() | |
| System | net_connect() | |
| System | checkPrivilege() | |

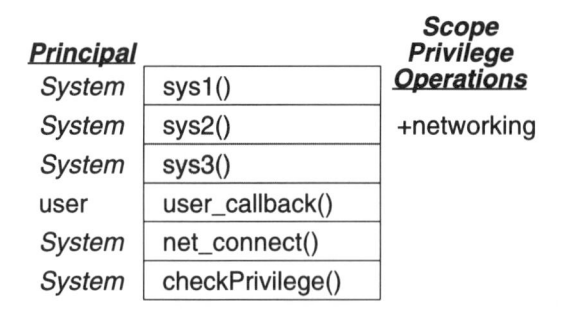

FIGURE 7. Untrusted code attempts to insert itself between a change of privilege and the privileged operation. Even if sys3() does not explicitly reduce its privileges, user_callback() may not use them because its principal lacks sufficient privileges. Grey areas indicate enabled scope privileges.

This gives applets three ultimate ways to make a network connection: call through NetSrv1() and connect to the NetSrv machine, call into safe_net_connect() and connect to the host from which the applet was loaded, or request *networking* privileges for itself. There are no other ways to get scope privileges for the *networking* target, so there are no other ways to make a network connection.

3.5.4. *Luring attacks.* Our design prevents *luring attacks*, in which an attacker might take advantage of trusted code calling into untrusted code while it has a privilege enabled. This can occur, for instance, when a system thread calls back into a user class, which is common with Java's Abstract Window Toolkit (AWT).

A luring scenario is illustrated in Figure 7. The untrusted class user_callback() manages to insert itself between two pieces of trusted code.

Luring attacks do not work because the system automatically restricts the scope privileges of the callee so that they fit within the privileges permitted to the callee's class (see section 3.4.4). Thus no privilege can be "accidentally" passed from the trusted code into the untrusted code.

In the example, the scope privileges of sys3() are {*networking*}. However, since user_callback() is not trusted, the class privileges of user_callback are empty, and thus the scope privileges of the call to user_callback() are restricted to 0. When user_callback() calls net_connect(), the empty scope privileges are passed along, so the connection is not allowed. The untrusted user_callback() code cannot hijack the privileges of its caller.

## 4. Implementation details

We have implemented our design in Netscape Navigator 4.0, which is expected to appear on the market soon.

Our implementation is designed to be equivalent to the model discussed above. However, the implementation is optimized in several ways to improve performance and simplify the lives of the user and developer.

There are two main implementation issues to discuss: where policy comes from, and how scope privileges are computed.

**4.1. Determining policies.** As stated in the model, there are several sources of policies: the site administrator, the targets, and the user (see section 3.4.1).

The site administrator's policy is expressed using the browser's general site administration mechanisms, which also control many of the non-Java security decisions for the browser. The site administrator's policy is expressed as JavaScript code and the browser is configured to automatically load this code when it starts running. When the Java virtual machine needs to consult the site administrator's policy, it calls into this code. If the browser is using an HTTP proxy, the browser program will refuse to run without loading the site administration code designated by the proxy; this allows a site to make the use of site-specific security policies mandatory.

Some targets, such as parameterized targets (see section 3.3), are "smart" — they implement a Java method to pass judgement on principal privilege requests. This method is passed a principal and responds with *allowed*, *abstain*, or *forbidden*. "Dumb" targets implicitly answer *abstain* to every question. Smart targets are used both as parameterized targets as well as adding access control policies *below* an existing API. For example, the security check done by the `safe_net_connect()` call from of figure 4, could be implemented below the networking code, in the same way Java currently uses its `SecurityManager`.

The user's policy is represented by an access matrix [7] which is stored in persistent state; all entries are initially marked *empty*. When an applet starts running, it calls `enablePrivilege()` to ask for privileges to be granted to its principals. The existing policies are consulted and their results combined according to the consensus voting rule (with *empty* equivalent to *abstain*). If the user's policy entry is *empty* and the result of the combination is *forbidden*, the system answers *forbidden* without asking the user, since the user's decision cannot affect the result (see equation 2). If, however, the user's entry is *empty* and the combination results in *abstain*, the user is shown a dialog box to change his or her policy to *allowed*, *abstain*, or *forbidden*.

The difference between *empty* and *abstain* in a user's policy breaks down to how requests for privileges from untrusted principals are treated. If the user's policy is *empty*, the user does not yet have any policy, so it's reasonable to query the user. If the user's policy is *abstain*, the user has specifically stated that this principal will not get privileges and should be effectively ignored. A principal marked *forbidden* would behave the same as one marked *abstain* with the additional property that classes with this principal could never successfully request a *forbidden* target.

We deviate slightly from our model by introducing a notion of "user targets." These targets, often macro targets, have additional methods which return text suitable for presenting to a user. Only user targets are allowed to be presented to a user for authorization. The user implicitly answers *abstain* to all questions about non-user targets. We believe this simplifies the security dialogs for novice users by guaranteeing they will only see dialogs for "user-friendly" targets.

**4.2. Computing scope privileges.** Although the model speaks in terms of scope privileges being computed and passed along with every method call (see section 3.4.4), this would be inefficient in practice. We wanted the common case of method calls to have no additional overhead, so we chose to compute scope privilege information lazily — only when it is needed.

We do this by annotating the stack frames generated by Java method calls. Every call to `enablePrivilege()` or `disablePrivilege()` puts an annotation on the current stack frame, recording the call and its arguments. This allows us to reconstruct their effect on scope privileges later.

We also observe that there is no need to record the initial scope privileges passed into each method call, since they can be reconstructed later. The existing Java runtime system already labels each stack frame with its Java class; since each class contains a list of its principals, we can therefore figure out how the scope privileges will change with every method call. The combination of this preexisting stack information and the new stack annotations gives us enough information to completely reconstruct the scope privileges at every frame on the stack.

We can optimize further by observing that when checkPrivilege(S) is called, we only need to know the parts of the scope privileges that pertain to the targets in $S$. We may ignore other annotations on the stack. Also, when we call checkPrivilege(), we are only interested in the scope privileges of the current stack frame. Rather than starting at the beginning of the stack and working down to the current frame, we can start at the current frame and work our way backward until we have enough information to deduce the relevant parts of the current state.

Regardless, our implementation uses a fairly expensive checkPrivilege() operation — with worst case run-time proportional to the stack depth — to keep common method calls as cheap as possible. In practice, checkPrivilege() calls should only happen for "occasional" operations, such as opening a network connection, rather than "frequent" operations, such as reading and writing data on a connection. Once user code has an open connection (an instance of a Socket class), method calls on that class require no further security checks.

## 5. Related work

Since the late 1960's, computer systems have utilized hardware features to separate and protect programs, serving to increase system robustness against bugs as well as to prevent malicious programs from reading or corrupting unauthorized data. Current systems, such as Unix, base their security on memory-protection to separate tasks, and system calls as a safe way to cross protection boundaries. All current microprocessors support this mode of operation. Earlier machines had significantly more diversity among their security mechanisms. More recent software systems have revisited (and sometimes reinvented) these early mechanisms. Software protection mechanisms have been subjected to a great deal of recent scrutiny, and are expected to figure prominently in current and future systems.

**5.1. Historical systems.** The GE 645 introduced a hardware ring system [8], allowing a hierarchy of memory protection. With rings, an operating system can implement a security kernel, which must be tamper-proof with respect to the remainder of the kernel, as well as user processes [9]. Rings are also supported by some current microprocessors [10]. Using rings, Multics [3], provided calls into protected subsystems that appear to the programmer just like normal subroutine calls. After passing through a *call gate*, which checks the legality of the call, memory from the internal ring is available to the subroutine. To contrast, the Burroughs B5000 (which evolved into the Unisys A-series [11]) did not rely on any address-space protection. Instead, it relied on trusted compilers for generating safe code, and tagged memory objects and pointers for hardware-mediated access control. A memory reference on the Burroughs represented a capability. Without such a memory reference, no way existed for one program (as generated by a trusted compiler) to corrupt the memory of another one. Many capability-based architectures were built in the 1970's, such as the IBM System/38 (which evolved into the IBM AS/400) and the Intel iAPX 432 [12], as well as software-based schemes like Hydra [13]. Hydra, Multics, PSOS [14], and other such capability-based systems bear a striking resemblance to Java — pointers are unforgeable, private object memory is only accessible by specific subroutines, and posession of a reference to an object usually represents the privilege to use that reference.

While a complete comparison of these architectures is beyond the scope of this paper, it is useful to examine how they perform *amplification* of privilege. Ring-based systems allow a limited number of entry points into each of the successively more internal and privileged rings. Changing rings only incurs the costs normally associated with a subroutine call. Once a new ring has been entered, more pages or segments of memory are mapped into the running address space or otherwise marked accessible. Capability and object-based systems allow the holder of an unforgeable bit-string (a key) to pass this key as an argument to a privileged subsystem which then uses it. In capability-based hardware, these keys include pointers to physical resources [12]; if you have the key, you can use the resource. In the IBM System/38, a mechanism called *profile adoption* allows a procedure to optionally retain its owner's security profile, which is then merged with the caller's profile, allowing the creation of protected subsystems. Similar mechanisms exist in Hydra (*amplification templates*) and even in generic Unix (*set-uid binaries*). Lampson [15] also discusses how confinement relates to procedure calls.

**5.2. Recent systems.** Java and other systems like Telescript [16], Safe-Tcl [17], Phantom [18], and Juice [19], revisit the problem of defining and enforcing protection domains, but with the added wrinkle that they don't use any hardware memory protection to achieve it (although it may still be useful [20]). Software-based protection seems inevitable for its portability across operating systems and processors, its expressive flexibility, as well as its potential to outperform hardware-based schemes, particularly for fine-grained protection boundaries.[4] Where hardware-based schemes are fundamentally based on memory-mapping primitives (page-tables or segments), software-based schemes are based on language type-safety.

To enforce type-safety, Safe-Tcl and Telescript rely on dynamic run-time type information available in the interpreter. Java and Juice attempt to analyze their input statically, to remove many run-time checks. Phantom relies on a trusted type-safe compiler (on a trusted Internet host), which digitally signs its output. Necula and Lee [23] introduce the notion of *proof-carrying code*, where a program is shipped with a proof of its memory-safety, or of other properties. The proof, which can be generated by hand but may eventually be automatically generated by a compiler, can be quickly verified before execution, and imposes no run-time execution cost.

The system presented in this paper attempts to extend Java with a notion of principals, which may or may not be allowed to access targets in the system, depending on system policies with respect to the principals and stack-based runtime mechanisms. Telescript has a similar notion called *permits*, which grant or revoke privileges for a specific block of code; when the block exits, the privileges return to their previous state. Jaeger, Rubin, and Prakash [24] also discuss how flexible policies might be generally implemented in an interpreter.

**5.3. Java security.** To safely grant additional privileges to Java applets, we need to consider previous failures of Java's security. Dean, Felten, and Wallach [5] catalog and analyze a number of these attacks. More discussion on Java security can also be found

---

[4]Modern RISC processors take increasingly large penalties for context switching [21] — this could be much cheaper in a software-only system. Software-only protection creates opportunities for run-time optimizations [22], which may be able to further reduce the cost of crossing protection boundaries.

in [25, 26]. We can grossly break these attacks into three categories: type-safety exploits, class-library bug exploits, and unintended interactions with external systems.

- Type-safety exploits rely on subtle runtime bugs that allow unchecked type-casts. Subverting Java's type system allows an attacker to directly invoke private methods or even inject native machine code and cause it to be executed. An example of this is the family of ClassLoader attacks discussed in [5].
- Class-library bugs are simply unintended errors in the specification of the Java system libraries. An example of this was the System.out file-stream, stored in a non-final public variable in Netscape 2.x (changed to final in Netscape 3.x).[5] An attacker could replace the output stream with an arbitrary class, arrange for trusted code to print something, then trick the trusted code into acting inappropriately.
- Java's security policy does not always compose with external systems [27]. Java unnecessarily trusted the DNS which allowed an applet, in collusion with an external DNS server, to connect to any IP address, including those behind an organization's firewall. Likewise, some firewalls unnecessarily trust the FTP PORT command, which allows Java to open holes in some packet-filtering firewalls . While Java may be safe on its own, the Java security policy may rest on other systems with less security, such as DNS.

A remarkable amount of engineering effort has gone into addressing these problems, as successive releases of the major browsers have fixed bug after bug. Additionally, Java now has a separate language specification [28] and verification suite[6], partially addressing the previously ad-hoc penetrate-and-patch method used in analyzing Java. Historically, the entire runtime and class libraries must be correct for the system to be correct. Any bug, anywhere in the vendor-supplied Java system could have led to a collapse of system security. This contrasts with the security principle of minimizing the TCB [29].

## 6. Future work

This system only addresses permissions within a single Java virtual machine. Integrating this system with RPC security mechanisms [30] or authenticated network channels [31, 32] presents a number of interesting challenges.

While we have defined a new security system which appears to have interesting properties, it would be constructive to build formal models and reason about the system's security. For example, Dean [33] has modelled the Java dynamic linking mechanism and formally demonstrated the properties necessary for it to be safe.

Finally, extensive usability testing, which is now being carried out, and refinement will be necessary to truly make this system palatable to common users.

## 7. Conclusions

Users and developers have demanded that Java applets be granted privileges which might be abused if available to all applets. In response to this, we have designed a system for associating principals with classes in the Java runtime, managing which principals are allowed access to potentially dangerous resources, and limiting the exposure of these privileges to attackers. Both users and system administrators can express their policies either through simple security dialogs or general scripting mechanisms. This flexibility allows

---

[5] Java's System.out is similar to C's stdout. Java's final modifier is similar to C++'s const, when applied to variables.

[6] Java Compatibility Kit, available to Java licensees

trusted developers to step outside the Java "sandbox" and build real programs which access controlled system resources. Our design has been implemented in a commercial web browser, which is expected to be released soon.

## 8. Acknowledgments

Thanks to Raman Tenneti, Tom Dell and the Java group at Netscape for sharing the details of their design and supporting Dan Wallach as a visitng member of the design and implementation team. Thanks to Drew Dean, Dirk Balfanz, Li Gong, Ben Renaud, Marianne Mueller, Frank Yellin, Trent Jaeger, Rangachari Anand, and Nayeem Islam for many interesting conversations about our work.

Edward W. Felten is supported in part by an NSF National Young Investigator award.

## References

[1] Sun Microsystems, *Frequently Asked Questions - Applet Security*, 1995. http://java.sun.com/sfaq/.
[2] Microsoft Corporation, *Proposal for Authenticating Code Via the Internet*, Apr. 1996. http://www.microsoft.com/intdev/security/authcode/.
[3] J. H. Saltzer, "Information proection and the control of sharing in the Multics system," *Communications of the ACM*, vol. 17, pp. 388–402, July 1974.
[4] F. Yellin, "Low level security in Java," in *Fourth International World Wide Web Conference*, (Boston, MA), World Wide Web Consortium, Dec. 1995. http://www.w3.org/pub/Conferences/WWW4/Papers/197/40.html.
[5] D. Dean, E. W. Felten, and D. S. Wallach, "Java security: From HotJava to Netscape and beyond," in *Proceedings of the 1996 IEEE Symposium on Security and Privacy*, (Oakland, CA), pp. 190–200, May 1996.
[6] J. A. Goguen and J. Meseguer, "Security policies and security models," in *Proceedings of the 1982 IEEE Symposium on Security and Privacy*, (Oakland, CA), pp. 11–20, May 1982.
[7] B. W. Lampson, "Protection," in *Proceedings of the Fifth Princeton Symposium on Information Sciences and Systems*, (Princeton University), pp. 437–443, Mar. 1971. Reprinted in *Operating Systems Review*, 8(1):18–24, Jan. 1974.
[8] M. D. Schroeder and J. H. Saltzer, "A hardware architecture for implementing protection rings," *Communications of the ACM*, vol. 15, pp. 157–170, Mar. 1972.
[9] S. R. Ames, Jr., M. Gasser, and R. G. Schell, "Security kernel design and implementation: An introduction," *Computer*, pp. 14–22, July 1983. Reprinted in *Tutorial: Computer and Network Security*, M. D. Abrams and H. J. Podell, editors, IEEE Computer Society Press, 1987, pp. 142–157.
[10] D. A. Patterson and J. L. Hennessy, *Computer Architecture: a Quantitative Approach*. Morgan Kaufmann, 1990.
[11] Unisys Corporation, *Unisys A18 System Architecture MCP/AS (Extended): Support Reference Manual*, Apr. 1994. http://www.unisys.com/marketplace/aseries/pdf/70081781.pdf.
[12] H. M. Levy, *Capability-Based Computer Systems*. Digital Press, 1984.
[13] W. Wulf, E. Cohen, W. Corwin, A. Jones, R. Levin, C. Pierson, and F. Pollack, "HYDRA: The kernel of a multiprocessor operating system," *Communications of the ACM*, vol. 17, pp. 337–345, June 1974.
[14] P. G. Neumann, R. S. Boyer, R. J. Feiertag, K. N. Levitt, and L. Robinson, "A provably secure operating system: The system, its applications, and proofs," Tech. Rep. CSL-116, 2nd Ed., SRI International, May 1980.
[15] B. W. Lampson, "A note on the confinement problem," *Communications of the ACM*, vol. 16, pp. 613–615, Oct. 1973.
[16] General Magic, Inc., *The Telescript Language Reference*, Oct. 1995. http://www.genmagic.com/Telescript/TDE/TDEDOCS_HTML/telescript.html.
[17] N. S. Borenstein, "Email with a mind of its own: The Safe-Tcl language for enabled mail," in *IFIP International Working Conference on Upper Layer Protocols, Architectures and Applications*, 1994.
[18] A. Courtney, "Phantom: An interpreted language for distributed programming," in *USENIX Conference on Object-Oriented Technologies*, June 1995.
[19] M. Franz and T. Kistler, "Slim binaries," Tech. Rep. 96-24, University of California, Irvine, June 1996. http://www.ics.uci.edu/~franz/SlimBinaries-ics-tr-96-24.ps.

[20] I. Goldberg, D. Wagner, R. Thomas, and E. A. Brewer, "A secure environment for untrusted helper applications: Confining the wily hacker," in *Sixth USENIX Security Symposium Proceedings*, (San Jose, CA), pp. 1–12, July 1996.

[21] T. E. Anderson, H. M. Levy, B. N. Bershad, and E. D. Lazowska, "The interaction of architecture and operating system design," in *Proceedings of the Fourth ACM Symposium on Architectural Support for Programming Languages and Operating Systems*, 1991.

[22] C. Chambers, *The Design and Implementation of the Self Compiler, an Optimizing Compiler for Object-Oriented Programming Languages*. PhD thesis, Stanford University, 1992. http://self.smli.com/papers/craig-thesis.html.

[23] G. C. Necula and P. Lee, "Safe kernel extensions without run-time checking," in *Second Symposium on Operating Systems Design and Implementation (OSDI '96) Proceedings*, (Seattle, WA), pp. 229–243, Oct. 1996.

[24] T. Jaeger, A. D. Rubin, and A. Prakash, "Building systems that flexibly control downloaded executable content," in *Sixth USENIX Security Symposium Proceedings*, (San Jose, CA), pp. 131–148, July 1996.

[25] M. Weiss, A. Johnson, and J. Kiniry, "Security features of Java and HotJava," tech. rep., Open Software Foundation Research Institute, Mar. 1996. http://www.osf.org/mall/web/SW-java/security.htm.

[26] G. McGraw and E. W. Felten, *Java Security: Hostile Applets, Holes, and Antidotes*. John Wiley and Sons, 1996.

[27] D. M. Martin Jr., S. Rajagopalan, and A. D. Rubin, "Blocking Java applets at the firewall," in *Internet Society Symposium on Network and Distributed System Security (NDSS '97)*, (San Diego, CA), 1997.

[28] J. Gosling, B. Joy, and G. Steele, *The Java Language Specification*. Addison-Wesley, 1996.

[29] National Computer Security Center, *Department of Defense Trusted Computer System Evaluation Criteria (The Orange Book)*. 1985.

[30] J. Siegel, ed., *CORBA Fundamentals and Programming*. John Wiley and Sons, 1996.

[31] E. Wobber, M. Abadi, M. Burrows, and B. Lampson, "Authentication in the Taos operating system," *ACM Transactions on Computer Systems*, vol. 12, pp. 3–32, Feb. 1994.

[32] A. O. Freier, P. Karlton, and P. C. Kocher, *The SSL Protocol: Version 3.0*, Mar. 1996. Internet draft, ftp://ietf.cnri.reston.va.us/internet-drafts/draft-freier-ssl-version3-%01.txt.

[33] D. Dean, "The security of static typing with dynamic linking," in *Fourth ACM Conference on Computer and Communications Security*, (Zurich, Switzerland), Apr. 1997.

[34] J. P. Anderson, "Computer security technology planning study," Tech. Rep. ESD-TR-73-51, U.S. Air Force, Electronic Systems Division, Deputy for Command and Management Systems, HQ Electronic Systems Division (AFSC), L. G. Hanscom Field, Bedford, MA 01730 USA, Oct. 1972. Volume 2, pages 58–69.

**For more information related to this paper, please visit our web page:**
http://www.cs.princeton.edu/sip/

DEPARTMENT OF COMPUTER SCIENCE, PRINCETON UNIVERSITY, 35 OLDEN STREET, PRINCETON, NJ 08544

# Trust and Security: A New Look at the Byzantine Generals Problem

Mike Burmester, Yvo Desmedt, and Gregory Kabatianski

ABSTRACT. Secure communication in an open dynamic network in the presence of a malicious adversary is central to secure distributed computation. We address this issue. First we link the notion of trust with security, by regarding trust as a mechanism for authentication. The trust-graph is a graph with vertices the processors, whose edges correspond to trusting pairs of processors. Our model is computational, and we assume that there is a bound $u$ on the number of faulty (malicious) processors, and that the trust-graph is $(2u + 1)$-connected.

In this paper we focus on the case when the trust depends on shared secret keys and conventional authentication is used (without signatures). We use a modular approach in which authentication is based on a two-party authentication protocol. We regard this as a primitive. It is easy to see that if the sender and receiver both know the trust-graph then they can communicate securely (as securely as the primitive). However if only the sender knows the trust-graph, then we do not know of any way of finding secure paths, other than by exhaustive search. The problem of secure communication for this case is related to two **NP**-complete problems. It is not clear if it is **NP**-complete.

## 1. Introduction

Secure communication in an open and dynamic network system (such as the internet) in the presence of a malicious adversary is central to secure distributed computation. By using an authentication protocol the power of the adversary can be restricted, however the problem is that the sender may not share a secret key with (or know the public-key of) the receiver. Finding authentication paths through intermediary processors may not be possible if the sender does not know which pairs of processors can authenticate messages. In this paper we address this issue. We motivate our discussion by considering an extension of the classic Byzantine generals problem which is open and dynamic: generals come and go, with newcomers not recognized by some, those staying not knowing who left.

First we discuss the notion of trust, from an abstract point of view, by regarding it as key for authentication mechanisms, or as a probability to forward such keys, or more generally as a boolean expression. We represent the trust relationship between processors by a trust-graph whose edges correspond to trusting pairs. We

---

1991 *Mathematics Subject Classification.* Primary 68M10, 90B12, 68M15; Secondary 68R10, 68Q25.

The third author was supported by an EPSRC Visiting Fellowship grant (GR/L 209000).

© 1998 American Mathematical Society

then consider the problem of secure communication in an open dynamic network system which is reliable and synchronous. We use a computational model, and assume that the number of faulty (malicious) processors is bounded by $u$, and that the trust-graph is $(2u + 1)$-connected.

In this paper we focus on the case when the trust depends on shared secret keys and conventional authentication is used. We use a modular approach, with the authentication based on a two-party authentication protocol which we regard as a primitive. The reason for this is practicality: there are currently available several two-party authentication protocols for which we have a good tradeoff between efficiency and security (*e.g.* [1]). It is easy to see that the sender and receiver can communicate securely if they both know the trust-graph. In this case the security is as strong as the primitive. However if the trust-graph is known to the sender but not the receiver, then the problem of secure communication is related to two **NP**-complete problems. It is not clear whether this problem is **NP**-complete. Indeed we do not know of any way of solving it, other than by exhaustive search.

The organization of this paper is as follows. In Section 2 we motivate our general model of trust and secure communication using an extended version of the Byzantine generals paradigm. In Section 3 we consider various models of trust, and in Section 4 we address the issue of secure communication for various scenaria. We conclude in Section 5 with remarks.

**Related work.** There are many papers in the literature which analyze various aspects the notion of trust. Recent work, similar to ours, is by Beth-Borcherding-Klein [3] and Maurer [12]. However there are differences with our model, and our results are more general. Reiter-Stubblebine [15] consider trust-paths, for authentication, as we do. Our results are for a general model. Part of our work is based on earlier results presented at DIMACS [5].

Perlman [10, pp. 462–465] describes a different jamming attack and a solution based on certificates originating from a certifying authority. We do not have a certifying authority and so her solution can not be used.

## 2. The Byzantine generals paradigm: a motivation for a general model of trust and secure communication

In the classic Byzantine generals paradigm [14, 11] a city is surrounded by Byzantine forces and their generals. Generals can communicate either directly, or indirectly through other generals, orally or in writing using messengers. The messengers are reliable and loyal. A general wants to send a message to the others. However some generals are traitorous and want to prevent the other generals from agreeing on which message was sent. These generals may conspire and follow a malevolent plan.

Recognition, whether oral or written, can be regarded as a bond of *trust* which links the parties involved: if general $g_i$ recognizes general $g_j$ (or his signature), then $g_i$ trusts that $g_j$ is who he is suppose to be (whether loyal or traitorous). The trust among the generals can be represented by a *trust-graph* whose vertices $g_i$ correspond to the generals, and for which $(g_i, g_j)$ is an edge if $g_i$ recognizes $g_j$ (the edge is directed if the trust is not mutual). In the classic Byzantine paradigm, each general recognizes the others (or their signatures) and there is complete interconnection. That is, the trust-graph is a complete graph. A weaker requirement would be near-completeness: one or more of the generals may be "trusted third parties", *i.e.* known to be loyal and recognized by (almost) all the others. However even this setting is not suitable for large open and dynamic networks such as the internet. In our extended paradigm we allow for the following aspects:

- *Open network*: No *a priori* assumption is made about the trust-graph of the generals, *i.e.* about who (or whose signature) is recognized by whom. There may be several generals which a particular general has not met before (or whose signature he does not recognize).
- *Dynamic setting*: No *a priori* assumption is made about knowledge of the trust-graph by the generals. New generals may join the task force. A general may not recognize them (or their signatures), and may not know any other general who recognizes them (or their signatures). If generals leave, others may not be aware of this.
- *Subset consensus*: A consensus may be required from a subset of loyal generals. If the subset consists of a sender and receiver only, and both are loyal, we require secure communication (this is not trivial in the extended paradigm).

In this paradigm, communication between generals $g_{i_1}$ and $g_{i_n}$ may only be possible indirectly through intermediary generals who trust each other. In an oral communication (authentication without signatures) the messages sent are of type: "general $g_{i_{n-2}}$ told me that, general $g_{i_{n-3}}$ told him that, ..., general $g_{i_1}$ (the sender) said, attack". These should include the path to be followed: $g_{i_1}, g_{i_2}, \ldots, g_{i_n}$, as specified by the sender (and a sequence number). The message would be delivered orally to general $g_{i_n}$ (the receiver) by general $g_{i_{n-1}}$. All pairs of generals $(g_{i_j}, g_{i_{j+1}})$ in the trust-path should recognize each other. With written messages, general $g_{i_1}$ (the sender) signs his message, and then in turn, each general $g_{i_j}$ in the path signs the message, to confirm its authenticity. In this case, each general $g_{i_{j+1}}$ must recognize the signature of the previous signer $g_{i_j}$. In both cases, only the last authentication step can be verified by the receiver. So traitorous generals may create bogus paths.

**Applications.**
1. *Secure network communication.*
2. *Fault-tolerant network systems.* The classic example is of a flight control system which uses the feedback from various physical sensors. The sensor values have to be distributed to each processor. The data can be replicated, but the replicates may not be identical. For fault-tolerance, the system should operate in the presence of faults (which could be malicious).

## 3. Models for trust

The notion of trust is intangible, even though it is an essential ingredient for the design of secure protocols. Trust comes in different flavors. If Bob shares a secret key with Alice then he trusts that all messages authenticated with this key are Alice's. If Bob knows Alice's public-key then he trusts that all signed messages that he can verify with this key are Alice's. In both cases the trust of Bob is based on the knowledge of a key: it is symmetric in the first case, but not necessarily so in the second. Although trust is usually assumed to be transitive [4], there is no reason why this should be so in the general case. In the models we consider, we deal with a very general kind of trust which is not absolute but *relative*. For example, if the trust is based on physical recognition then the fact that Bob recognizes Alice, and that Carol recognizes Bob, does not imply that Carol recognizes Alice. If Alice tells Bob that she believes statement $x$, then Bob trusts that: "Alice believes $x$". Bob's trust is based on his ability to recognize others. If Bob tells Carol that "Alice believes $x$" then Carol trusts that: "Bob said that, Alice believes $x$" is true. Not that: "Alice believes $x$" is true. Indeed Bob may have lied.

**The trust-graph.** It is futile to attempt to define in any particular way the trust relationship. Instead we describe several models for it. First we represent it by a graph, the *trust-graph*, whose vertices $A, B, \ldots$ correspond to the processors, with $(A, B)$ an edge if $B$ trusts $A$. The edge is undirected if the relation is symmetric, otherwise it is directed, see Figure 1. In Figure 2 there are two trust paths from $A$ to $B$.

FIGURE 1. Bob trusts Alice: the symmetric and non-symmetric case.

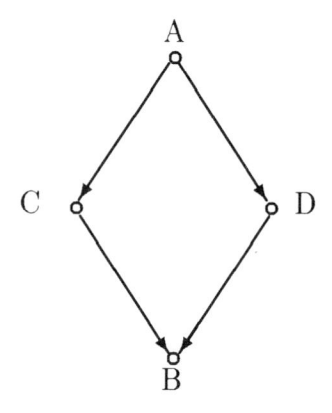

FIGURE 2. The trust of Bob in Alice is sustained by two trust-paths.

**3.1. A Boolean model.** We view the trust between two processors as a Boolean expression induced by the trust-graph. In this model the vertices are Boolean variables. If $B$ and $A$ are adjacent, the trust of $B$ in $A$ is 1. In Figure 3 the trust of $B$ in $A$ is: $C \wedge D$.

FIGURE 3. The trust of $B$ in $A$ with one trust-path.

For Figure 2 the trust of $B$ in $A$ is the Boolean expression: $C \vee D$. In Figure 4 there are three intersecting paths from $A$ to $B$. In this case the trust of $B$ in $A$ is:
$$(C \wedge E) \vee (D \wedge F) \vee (C \wedge F).$$

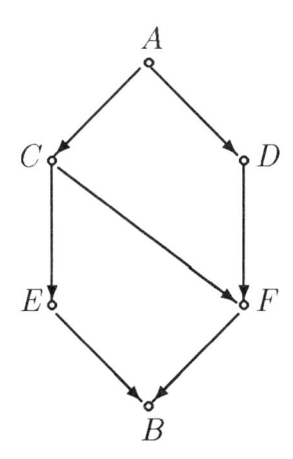

FIGURE 4. The trust of $B$ in $A$ with overlapping trust-paths.

**3.2. A Probabilistic model.** In this model trust is a probability. We assign to each vertex $X$ of the trust-graph, independently, a probability $p_X$. We regard $p_X$ as the probability that process $X$ will forward correctly the public-key of a neighbor. In this model the trust of $B$ in $A$ is the probability that $B$ will get the correct key from $A$. For the graph in Figure 2, the probability that $B$ will be get the correct key from $A$ is: $p_C + (1 - p_C)p_D$. Similarly the probability that $B$ will be get the correct key from $A$ in Figure 3 is: $p_C \cdot p_D$. In Figure 4 it is: $p_C p_F + (1 - p_C)p_D p_F + (1 - p_F)p_C p_E$.

**3.3. A Deterministic model.** For this model the trust is restricted to the trust-graph. As in the other models, the trust may be based on possession of a key. For example, $B$ shall trust $A$ if, $B$ possesses a certified public-key of $A$. We have an undirected edge if $A, B$ share a secret key.

We shall use this basic model in the following sections to study the security of networks. Our task will be to investigate the possibility of achieving secure communication in the presence of a malicious adversary.

## 4. Secure communication

It is claimed in the literature that secure communication can be achieved in a reliable synchronous network system if appropriate cryptographic tools are used (*e.g.*, [11]). This result is proved in the case when the trust-graph is a complete graph, or a nearly complete graph. The proof uses techniques from network reliability.

In this paper we address the general case when the trust-graph is not necessarily known to the processors in the network, and when the only assumption on its topology is a certain degree of connectivity. We focus on the case when the trust depends on conventional authentication without signatures, *e.g.* with Message Authentication Codes [13], and use a modular approach in which authentication is based on a two-party authentication protocol. We take this as a primitive. The security of the scheme is therefore based on the security of the primitive.

Before we proceed with our analysis, we clarify our setting and the role of the adversary. In the next sections we shall make the following assumptions on the network system.

- *Reliability*: All processors can communicate reliably.[1]
- *Synchrony*: There is an upper bound on the possible delay of sending or receiving a message. We allow for messages to be delivered in different order than sent (communication asynchrony), but assume that all non-faulty processors will respond within a certain time (process synchrony). Processors which go to sleep are treated as faulty, and under the control of the adversary.[2]
- *Bounds on resources*: Authentication can be established in polynomial time (in the number of processors in the network and a security parameter). Also, all processors, including the adversary are polynomially time bounded.

The adversary $E$ controls faulty processors, and may use a malicious plan. Her goal is to prevent the non-faulty processors from communicating securely. For this purpose $E$ can employ various strategies. If a message is to be authenticated through a path from processor $A$ to processor $B$ involving several intermediary processors, and if one of these is faulty, $E$ can create bogus paths to $B$ through which a bogus message is authenticated.

To achieve secure communication in this scenario, we put a bound $u$ on the number of faulty processors, and have the sender authenticate the message through $2u+1$ vertex-disjoint paths. This is a standard technique used in network reliability. In the following sections we shall see how this technique can be used for our purpose.

**4.1. The trust-graph is known to the sender and receiver.** Then we get secure communication if the connectivity of the trust-graph is greater than $2u$. This result holds for both the public-key case and the secret-key case. For the sake of simplicity we assume that the trust is based on sharing secret keys, and that a conventional cryptosystem is used as the primitive for authentication. Let $k_{XY}$ be the secret key shared by $X$ and $Y$.

ALGORITHM 4.1. Processor $A$ authenticates a message $m$ to $B$
Suppose that the number of faulty processors is no more than $u$ and that, if $A, B$ are non-adjacent, there are at least $(2u + 1)$ vertex-disjoint paths from $A$ to $B$.

1. If $A, B$ are adjacent, $A$ authenticates $m$ to $B$ directly. Otherwise $A$ finds $2u + 1$ vertex-disjoint paths using an appropriate deterministic (max-flow based) algorithm [8], and chooses the first $2u+1$ paths (*e.g.* in lexicographical order),

$$\pi_i = (A = A_{i_0}, A_{i_1}, A_{i_2}, \ldots, A_{i_{t(i)+1}} = B), \quad i = 1, 2, \ldots, 2u+1,$$

and authenticates to each processor $A_{i_1}$ the pair $(\pi_i, m)$.[3] The message $m$ includes a sequence number.

---

[1] We assume that appropriate anti-jamming techniques are used to prevent the adversary from jamming messages.

[2] The adversary can always arrange for faulty processors to sent bogus messages. However he cannot corrupt a message sent by a non-faulty processor, or prevent it from being received.

[3] If Message Authentication Codes [13] are used, $A$ sends $(\pi, m, MAC(k_{A,A_1}, \pi_i, m))$ to $A_{i_1}$.

2. Each processor $A_{i_j}$ different from $A$ and $B$ which receives $(\pi_i, m)$ authenticated by $A_{i_{j-1}}$ accepts it, if it has been authenticated[4] with the shared key $k_{A_{i_{j-1}}, A_{i_j}}$, and if $\pi_i$ is a path in the trust-graph, and will authenticate $(\pi_i, m)$ to the next processor $A_{i_{j+1}}$ in the path. If $A_{i_j}$ does not accept $(\pi_i, m)$, it will not forward it.
3. The receiver $B$ finds the same $2u + 1$ vertex-disjoint paths as $A$, using the deterministic algorithm of $A$. When $B$ receives $(\pi_i, m)$ authenticated by $A_{i_{t(i)}}$, it will accept it, if it was authenticated with the key $k_{A_{i_{t(i)}}, B}$ that $B$ shares with it, and if $\pi_i$ is one of the computed paths. $B$ obtains the message by majority vote on the received authenticated messages.

CLAIM 4.2. *Suppose that the conditions in Section 4 hold, and that the trust-graph is known to $A$ and $B$. If $A, B$ are adjacent, or if there are $2u+1$ vertex-disjoint paths from $A$ to $B$, where $u$ is an upper bound on the number of faulty processors, then $A$ and $B$ can communicate securely.*

REMARK 4.3. The communication is as secure as the primitive two-party authentication system which is used. It is interesting to compare this protocol with other protocols for this scenario (when the trust-graph is known), *e.g.* the Secure Message Transmission protocol in [7], for which we have perfect secrecy and perfect resiliency.

**4.2. Conventional authentication (without signatures): the trust-graph is known to the sender but not the receiver.** Suppose that, as in the previous case, the sender $A$ authenticates to (a non-adjacent) receiver $B$ through $2u + 1$ vertex-disjoint paths a message $m$. Then $B$ will receive pairs of type $(\pi, m)$, where $\pi = (A = A_0, A_1, \ldots, A_{t+1} = B)$ is a path from $A$ to $B$ in the trust-graph, authenticated as in Algorithm 4.1. Every non-faulty processor $A_i$ in the path $\pi$ will verify that $(\pi, m)$ came from (or via) $A_{i-1}$ by checking its authenticity, using the shared key. If this check fails, $(\pi, m)$ will not be forwarded nor accepted.

Let us now discuss bogus paths. A bogus paths is a path which originates from a faulty processor, say $A_{i-1}$, which claims that it originated from $A_0$, via some $A_1$, etc (or some other subpath leading to $A_{i-1}$). A bogus path need not be a path of the trust-graph. A message traveling via a bogus path will be forwarded by a non-faulty processor $A_i$ to $A_{i+1}$ provided that: ($i$) the edges $(A_{i-1}, A_i)$ and $(A_i, A_{i+1})$ in the specified bogus path are edges in the trust-graph, ($ii$) $A_{i-1}$ has authenticated $(\pi, m)$ to $A_i$ using the key they share. The actual message $m$ (without the path specification) may be identical to an authentic one, but sent via a bogus path, or may be different. If the message $m$ originated from the sender $A$, *i.e.* if *it is authentic*, then it will be received by $B$ through at least $u + 1$ disjoint paths, and possibly many other bogus paths. Bogus paths must include at least one faulty processor. So, if the message did not originate from $A$, *i.e.* if it *is not authentic*, its path must go through at least one of a set of at most $u$ vertices corresponding to the faulty processors.

The problem of detecting authentic messages corresponds to the **NP**-complete Set Packing problem [9, #SP3 p.221]. The problem of detecting non-authentic messages corresponds to the **NP**-complete Hitting Set problem [9, #SP8 p.222].

---

[4]With Message Authentication Codes, processor $A_{i_{j-1}}$ checks that $k_{A_{i_{j-1}}, A_{i_j}}$ was used in $MAC(k_{A_{i_{j-1}}, A_{i_j}}, \pi_i, m)$.

However, since we know that the paths will be restricted to one type or the other (the number of faulty processors is at most $u$), it is not obvious to conclude whether our problem is **NP**-complete.

We do not know how to solve this problem, other than by exhaustive search, and definitely not when the sender also does not know the network graph, as is often the case in large open networks. We doubt if secure communication is possible when conventional authentication is used with symmetric keys, if the trust-graph is not known and if several insiders are dishonest.

## 5. Conclusion

We have analyzed the notion of trust in the context of network security by regarding it as a mechanism for authentication, and addressed the issue of secure communication in an open and dynamic network, using a computational model.

We have shown that if trust depends on shared secret keys and there are no more than $u$ faulty processors, and if the trust-graph is $(2u+1)$-connected and known to the sender but not the receiver, then the problem of secure communication is related to two **NP**-complete problems. We do not know of any way of solving this problem, other than by exhaustive search.

The case when the trust is based on public keys and the trust-graph is not known to the receiver will be discussed elsewhere.

*Acknowledgement.* We thank Mike Reiter and Stuart Stubblebine for discussions about certificates.

## References

[1] M. Bellare and P Rogaway, Entity Authentication and Key Distribution, Proceedings, *Advances in Cryptology - Crypto '93, Lecture Notes in Comput. Sci. vol. 773*, D. R. Stinson, Ed., Springer-Verlag, 1994, pp. 232–249.

[2] D. Bertsekas and R. Gallager, Data Networks, Prentice-Hall, NJ, 1992.

[3] T. Beth, M. Borcherding, and B. Klein, Valuation of trust in open networks, Proceedings, *Computer Security - Esorics 94, Lecture Notes in Comput. Sci. vol. 875*, D. Gollmann, Ed., Springer-Verlag, 1994, pp. 3–18.

[4] M. Burrows, M. Abadi and R. Needham, A logic of authentication, *ACM Trans. on Comput. Systems*, **8**(1) (1990), 18–36.

[5] Y. Desmedt and M. Burmester. Linking trust with Network reliability. Presented at DIMACS Workshop on Trust Management in Networks, South Plainfield, New Jersey, Sept 30 - Oct 2, 1996.

[6] D. Dolev. Unanimity in Unknown and Unreliable Environment, *IEEE 22nd Symp. on Found. of Comput. Science*, Oct 1981, pp. 159–168.

[7] D. Dolev, C. Dwork, O. Waarts and M. Yung. Perfectly Secure Message Transmission. *Journal of ACM*, **40**(1) (1993), 17–47.

[8] S. Even. *Graph algorithms*. Computer Science Press, Rockville, Maryland, 1979.

[9] M. R. Garey and D. S. Johnson. *Computers and Intractability: A Guide to the Theory of NP-Completeness*. W. H. Freeman and Company, San Francisco, 1979.

[10] C. Kaufman, R. Perlman and M. Speciner, *Network Security*, Prentice-Hall, Englewood Cliffs, New Jersey, 1995.

[11] L. Lamport, R. Shostak and M. Pease, The Byzantine Generals Problem, *Journal of ACM* **32**(2) (1982), 374–382.

[12] U. Maurer. Modeling public-key infrastructure, Proceedings, *Computer Security - Esorics 96, Lecture Notes in Comput. Sci. vol. 1146* E. Bertino, H. Kurth, G. Martella, E. Montolivo, Eds., Springer-Verlag, 1996, pp. 325–350.

[13] A. Menezes, P.C. van Oorschot and S.A. Vanstone, Handbook of Applied Cryptography, CRC Press, 1996.

[14] M. Pease, R. Shostak and L. Lamport, Reaching Agreement in the Presence of Faults, *Journal of ACM* **27**(2) (1980), 228–234.
[15] M. Reiter and S. Stubblebine, PathServer. Presented at DIMACS Workshop on Trust Management in Networks, South Plainfield, New Jersey, Sept 30 - Oct 2, 1996.

INFORMATION SECURITY GROUP, DEPT. OF MATHEMATICS, ROYAL HOLLOWAY, UNIVERSITY OF LONDON, EGHAM, SURREY TW20 OEX, U.K.
*E-mail address*: m.burmester@rhbnc.ac.uk

CENTER FOR CRYPTOGRAPHY, COMPUTER AND NETWORK SECURITY, DEPT. EE AND CS, UNIVERSITY OF WISCONSIN – MILWAUKEE, P.O. BOX 784, WI 53201 MILWAUKEE
*E-mail address*: desmedt@cs.uwm.edu

INSTITUTE FOR PROBLEMS OF INFORMATION TRANSMISSION, RUSSIAN ACADEMY OF SCIENCES, ERMOLOVOY 19, MOSCOW, GSP-4, RUSSIA
*E-mail address*: kaba@ippi.ac.msk.su

# Channels: Avoiding Unwanted Electronic Mail

## Robert J. Hall

**Abstract.** Receiving unwanted communications ranges from mere nuisance (junk mail) through annoyance (telemarketing) to actually endangering the usefulness of the medium (junk fax, obscene or harassing telephone calls). The usefulness of electronic mail is seriously threatened by the exploding commercialization of the Internet, because it is easy to collect and maintain address lists and cheap to mass-distribute messages. This paper describes a novel mechanism, *electronic mail channels*, that enables users to control who can send them messages, allowing preferential levels of access. The key idea is to give each user the capability of having arbitrarily many structured user names, each of which contains encoded within it a cryptographically secure (i.e., unguessable) random string. This paper also describes the implementation of a *personal channel agent* that makes channelized email as easy to use as ordinary email and facilitates administration operations, such as secure remote channel switching.

## 1 Introduction

Receiving unwanted communications ranges from mere nuisance (junk mail) through annoyance (telemarketing) to actually endangering the usefulness of the medium (junk fax, obscene or harassing telephone calls). The usefulness of electronic mail (email) is seriously threatened by commercialization of the Internet, because it is easier than ever to collect address lists and cheaper than ever to mass-distribute messages. If companies were to spend the same amount sending junk email as they do sending junk physical mail, one would likely get more than a hundred junk messages per day. Every time a user sends to a public mailing list or newsgroup, fills out a web form, or mails in a product registration card, the server cheaply obtains an email address and usually some indication of the user's interests. This information is sold to marketing firms who can easily automate mass emailings of advertisements, surveys, and other annoyances that cost the user connect time and, worse, valuable attention span. More sinister unwanted email is becoming common as well, such as harassment and hate mail.

---

1991 *Mathematics Subject Classification.* Primary 68N99.

Portions of this paper appear in a shorter article (copyright © ACM) by the same name that will appear in *Communications of the ACM*.

© 1998 AT&T Corp.

The primary technique used today for avoiding unwanted communication is to restrict the set of people to whom one gives one's address. For example, people pay to avoid having their phone numbers listed; in email, people sometimes maintain multiple email accounts, using different accounts for different purposes, such as commercial versus personal. This "unlisted address" approach is expensive and slow to recover from security breaches: if an address is leaked to an adversary, the only alternative is to pay the service provider to change it (often, a lengthy process). Once the address is changed, the customer must notify all legitimate correspondents of the change while keeping it from the adversary. Leaks of physical mail addresses can be crudely located by systematically varying the address slightly as it is given to different correspondents, for example, using a different nickname or middle initial when filling out forms. When a correspondent leaks a variant, such as through selling a mailing list, the user can deduce it from the address used on ensuing unwanted messages. This technique is limited because even though a leak can be traced, there is little that can be done to cut off the resulting unwanted communications.

This paper presents a novel technique, *electronic mail channels*, that builds on and systematizes these ideas in the domain of electronic mail communications. The approach solves the problems mentioned above for unlisted numbers and physical mail addresses, as well as additional problems introduced by the nature of email, providing a light-weight, fine-grained access control method. Essentially, each user's email account is made accessible via a user-controlled set of channels. Each channel has a distinct structured address which contains within it the account name and a cryptographically secure, i.e. unguessable, pseudorandom security string, known as a *channel identifier*. Each legitimate correspondent is allowed to know one of these access addresses. The account owner is provided simple controls for opening a new channel, closing a channel, and switching a channel by notifying selected correspondents of a new channel that is replacing the current one.

Using email channels raises a host of potential complexities for the user, including security, ease of use, and administration. To deal with these, I have designed and implemented an automated *personal channel agent (PCA)* that shields the user from most of these complexities; in typical daily usage, channelized email looks and feels to the users exactly like traditional email, while the user needs only infrequently to access the extra administrative controls mentioned above.

This paper is structured as follows. Section 2 discusses the design and applications of channel addresses; Section 3 discusses the complexities of using channel addresses, and describes the personal channel agent which is designed to manage them. Section 4 describes solutions to the channel switching problem under varying security assumptions. Final sections discuss limitations and future work, and compare channels to alternative approaches.

## 2  Channelized Addresses

A *channelized address* is an email address of the form

```
Username-ChannelID-@Host
```

An example is `hall-1xyz6q6py4-@research.att.com`, where the username is `hall`, the channel ID is "`1xyz6q6py4`", and the host is `research.att.com`. Note that this contains both traditional address information, such as host and user names, as well as an unguessable *channel identifier*. The user `hall` will typically allocate and open a number of these addresses, differing only in the channel ID, for different correspondents. The goal is to control the access of potential correspondents, not to ensure anonymity of the account owner, nor to guarantee privacy of the messages.

## 2.1 Channel Identifiers

Each channel identifier has two parts, a *security string* and a *channel class indicator*. It is critical that channel identifiers be practically *unguessable*, even when an adversary knows several of the user's other channel identifiers. Thus, the prototype generates security strings pseudorandomly using the cryptographically secure BlumBlumShub (BBS) generator[1], with a modulus size larger than 1024 bits. See [13] for other candidate generators. A channel ID contains 45 pseudorandom bits. This length implies that if a user maintains 128 ($2^7$) open channels, an adversary has one chance in $2^{45-7}$ (about 275 billion) of guessing an open channel with one message. A brute force attack, sending more than 100 billion messages to the same host, is impractical in today's Internet. Moreover, the security of BBS[1] implies that adversaries knowing previously generated bits have essentially no advantage in guessing further bits.

Due to character set restrictions in Internet mail protocols, the 45 pseudorandom bits are encoded into strictly alphanumeric ASCII characters 5 bits at a time, using only one case of the alphabet and the digits 3 through 8. I use this "base 32" scheme rather than the more standard base64 encoding, because the latter uses both cases of the alphabet, and not all mail systems on the internet maintain the alphabetic case of header fields. When a message is received, alphabetic case is ignored in comparing the channel ID to those of active channels.

The channel class indicates how mail on that channel will be treated by the recipient. Currently, the prototype implements the following three classes: Class 0 indicates a *send-only* channel, i.e., one which is permanently closed. These are useful when one wants to send a message to a public or adversarial address without giving away any access at all. Class 1 indicates a *private* channel, which means that the user expects mail from a known set of correspondents on it. Mail from other correspondents may be ignored on such a channel. Class 2 indicates a *public* channel, meaning that previously unknown correspondents may send on it. In the future, I plan on implementing a richer class scheme, including the following classes: 0 – SendOnly, 1 – Private, 2 – Permanent Public, 3 – Temporary Public, 4 – Commercial, and 9 – Introductory (see below).

Thus, a channel identifier has form `Cxxxxxxxx`, where `C` is a digit indicating the class and the `x`s encode the security string.

## 2.2 Applications

The multiple channels idea has several applications. For example, how can one participate in a public forum, such as a mailing list, without giving away access?

At subscription time, the user sends a public channel address to the list maintainer. All messages sent to the list will be delivered to the user on this channel. To send a message to the list itself, however, one uses a send-only return address. Anyone wishing to reply must send to the entire list.

If one wishes to allow private replies, one can allocate a *limited-lifetime* public channel and use it as the return address, perhaps explicitly indicating when it will be deactivated. People wishing to respond to the post can do so privately for a short while, but firms collecting interest-based mailing lists will be left with closed channels after the timeout period. The user can always choose to "upgrade" a correspondent to a permanent channel once contact is made.

Channels and list servers together can be used to implement *private mailing lists*, allowing groups to confer (a) without requiring that they all have direct channels to each other; and (b) while prohibiting outsiders from sending to the group. The idea is simply to establish a list server with an unguessable address known only to list members. Note that list members need not have direct channels to each other, so this might be useful, for example, when a single buyer needs to have a group discussion, such as an auction, with vendors who are mutually adversarial.

Channelized email can also enhance the effectiveness of email agents and filters[6, 2], by providing a categorization based on which correspondents are presumed to know which channels. For example, when filling out a registration form for a product, one can use a particular public channel. The filter could be instructed to classify all traffic on that channel as lower priority than traffic on more personal channels. Furthermore, once electronic money becomes widely used, one can also implement *pay-per-view* channels. The idea here is that the channel agent will only accept a message on a pay-per-view channel if it is accompanied by enough e-money to pay for the user's time in viewing the message. This could again be used for advertising, surveys, and other potentially annoying junk mail. On an *authenticated channel*, the filter rejects messages that are not digitally signed[13, 5, 12] by an expected correspondent. Note that an authenticated channel could even have a *well-known* identifier such as 1AUTHENTIC since unauthenticated messages are discarded unseen.

Another useful synergy of channels and email agents is the idea of the *introductory channel*, which is a public, pay-per-view channel having a well-known address. Each channel user having a powerful filtering agent, such as the Andrew system's FLAMES language[2], can establish a well-known public channel identifier such as 9INTRODUCE. A message to user-9INTRODUCE-@host will be automatically handled as follows. If it does not contain an e-money payment of some reasonable fee (say, $1.00), then the following reply is sent:

```
Dear correspondent:

Since my automated assistant is not sure of your
intentions, please resend your message enclosing
$1.00 in e-money. I will then read the message and,
if you are really a friend or other non-commercial
correspondent, I will cheerfully refund the dollar.
Otherwise, I will read the message but keep the dollar.

-- Bob Hall's email access agent.
<copy of original included>
```

If the re-sent message is junk or otherwise inappropriate, then the user simply keeps the fee, while if it is a legitimate attempt at contact, the user refunds the fee. Such a channel address could be published in directories. The risk of unwanted email is reduced arbitrarily by setting an appropriate access fee for unknown correspondents, since there is presumably a price that advertisers will not pay for mass-mailings. Yet it still allows access to long-lost friends and relatives, since the fee will be immediately refunded in that case.

## 2.3 Implementation

It is easy to get one's mail server to allow channelized addresses flexibly. In the prototype (see Figure 1), a modified Unix sendmail[3] parses addresses, checking the user part in the system password file as usual, and matching the channel ID part (case-insensitively) against a list of open channels maintained in the user's channels file. The message is bounced if either the channel is not open or if there is no channel ID present in the address. In the future, the prototype will allow the user to specify the error message sent with any bounced messages; currently, the error is specified as "no permission." While this implementation is based on sendmail, analogous changes should be straight-forward for other mail processing systems.

## 2.4 Security

The success of the channels approach requires that the user's mail server, client machine, and the local network connecting them cannot be systematically eavesdropped by an adversary; otherwise, the eavesdropper would have access to all open channels appearing in the user's mail traffic. While this assumption of server-security may not hold in all cases, it is plausible, for example, when the server is run by a reputable commercial on-line service. In that case, the server and at least part of the network will be physically secured and administered competently. Moreover, users connect via modems over traditional voice lines, where eavesdropping requires relatively expensive hardware techniques, unlike connections over ethernet where peer hosts can freely snoop on the packet stream.

Note that the channels approach does *not* require that the entire network be impervious to eavesdropping. By giving correspondents individual access channels, the user can discover immediately which correspondent has breached security (either accidentally or by being eavesdropped). At that point, the user can either switch the channel, if the breach was a one-time occurrence, or else establish a cryptographically authenticated channel. (This authentication feature is not yet implemented in the prototype.)

# 3 The Personal Channel Agent

Maintaining multiple channels "manually" would be cumbersome and error-prone, leading to the following problems.

- *Return Address Problem.* Remembering what channel to use as your return address for a particular user would be onerous.

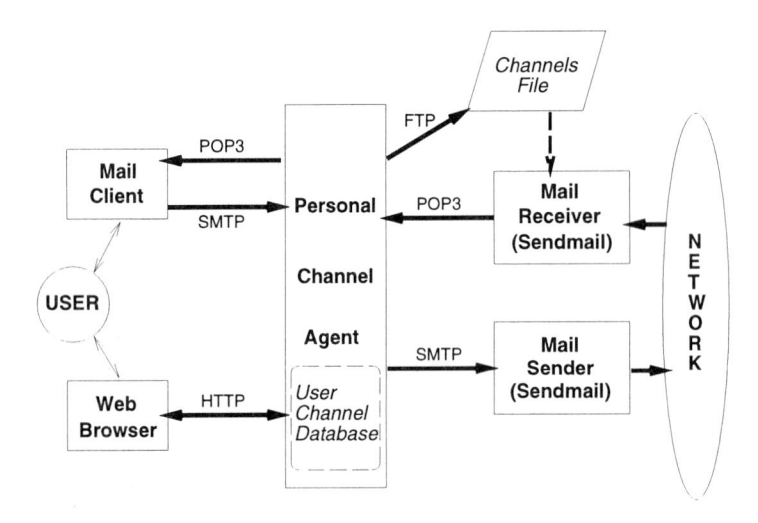

Figure 1: A block diagram of the Personal Channel Agent prototype.

- *Cc Problem.* When sending to multiple recipients, security is breached if one simply includes everyone's channelized addresses, since it is unlikely each reader will be authorized for each other's channel. For example, suppose one sends a message to a mailing list and cc's a friend's private channel address. The cc will be visible to all list readers, so they will all gain unauthorized access to the friend.

- *Reply/Forward Problem.* People frequently include a received message within a reply to or forward of it. If the message contains channel IDs, then the user must remember to edit them out in order to avoid leaks.

- *Anomaly Tracking.* It is useful to notice when users send on channels they are not authorized for so that leaks can be isolated when they become a problem. However, the problem may take a while to appear, as more and more junk traffic builds up on a channel, while the original leaks will be long forgotten.

This section describes the *Personal Channel Agent (PCA)* I have designed and implemented that manages these complexities on behalf of the user. After briefly describing the implementation, succeeding sections describe the PCA's primary functions.

## 3.1 PCA Implementation

Figure 1 shows how the PCA prototype fits into an email system. Conceptually, the PCA acts as an email proxy, sitting between the user's mail client and the mail server itself, with a web browser being used to administer the PCA. All PCA interfaces use standard protocols (SMTP[11], POP3[9], HTTP[4], FTP) to interact with clients and servers, so no special client software is needed to use it. This proxy

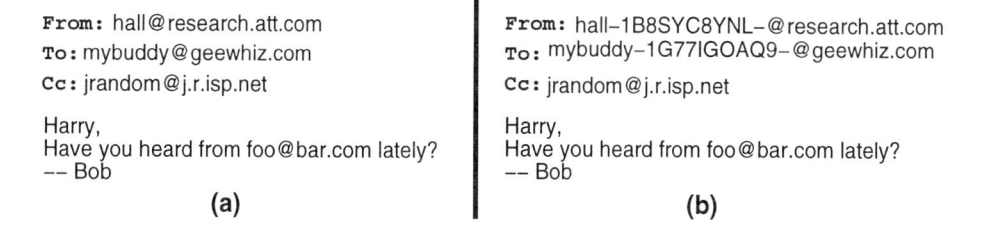

| | |
|---|---|
| From: hall@research.att.com<br>To: mybuddy@geewhiz.com<br>Cc: jrandom@j.r.isp.net<br><br>Harry,<br>Have you heard from foo@bar.com lately?<br>-- Bob<br>**(a)** | From: hall-1B8SYC8YNL-@research.att.com<br>To: mybuddy-1G77IGOAQ9-@geewhiz.com<br>Cc: jrandom@j.r.isp.net<br><br>Harry,<br>Have you heard from foo@bar.com lately?<br>-- Bob<br>**(b)** |

Figure 2: (a) Sending user sees this. (b) Actually transmitted to geewhiz.com.

positioning allows the PCA to perform bookkeeping functions autonomously, on both incoming and outgoing messages, shielding the user from them.

Note that this architecture allows the PCA to run on a host separate from the mail server's host, so that any additional computational load incurred by the PCA can be distributed. Alternatively, it could run on the same host if desired. The only additional load necessarily incurred by the mail server is in parsing the address (insignificant), plus the time to check the channels file. This is only significant for large channels files or slow file access. If users want to keep open many channels, the current flat file can be compiled by the PCA into a format supporting faster access.

A key part of the PCA is the *user channel database (UCDB)* which primarily records two mappings. The *channel map* associates each correspondent with the channel on which the user expects to receive mail from it. The *correspondent-address map* associates each correspondent's user and host names with the channel ID on which to send *to* the correspondent, if any. Note that in the current implementation each correspondent is allowed at most one channel. While at first it might appear desirable to allow multiple channels per correspondent (say, for different purposes), recall that the primary purpose of the channels mechanism is to deny access through denying knowledge. No security is gained by a single individual knowing two or more access channels for a correspondent. Instead, the logical separation of traffic from a single user can be implemented using existing email filtering techniques[6, 2]. In combined architectures, an extended UCDB could accommodate the needs of both channels and email filters by allowing multiple channels per correspondent; however, one channel must be designated as the default for use when rewriting header and envelope information in outgoing messages.

## 3.2 Address Rewriting

The PCA rewrites the header and envelope information of each message as it comes in or goes out, leaving the body unaltered. (See Figure 2.) For incoming messages, it removes channel IDs from all header addresses before serving the message to the client. This solves the reply/forward problem, because the header of the included original will contain no channel IDs.

For outgoing messages, the PCA inserts channel IDs before forwarding the message to the mail server. For a single-recipient message, the PCA simply obtains the appropriate to-channel and from-channel to use from the UCDB of the sender and puts them into the recipient and sender fields, respectively (both in the message headers and in the SMTP envelope). This solves the return address problem.

Figure 2 (a) shows the sending user's view in the mail client, while (b) shows what is actually transmitted and received. The receiving user will see (a) if s/he has a PCA and (b) if not.

Multi-recipient messages are copied once per recipient listed in the SMTP envelope, and each copy is tailored to that recipient as described above. This solves the cc problem, because each recipient receives exactly one copy of the message containing only information s/he already knows.

Thus, to the user virtually all messages appear without channel IDs, and hence email looks and feels like traditional email. I discuss in Section 5 the impact of channels on correspondents who do not use a PCA.

*Why Rewrite Headers at all?* Why not put channel IDs *only* into the envelope and not insert them into header lines at all? There are several reasons for this pertaining to interoperation with non-channel users and non-SMTP mailers as well as user convenience.

- A non-channel user expects a valid return address (in order to be able to use the client's reply command, for example) to appear in the From field of a message, so the PCA must include it.

- The non-channel user will put a channelized address in the To field when originating a message, leading to the return address and reply/forward problems when the message arrives at the recipient. Thus, the PCA must remove it.

- Some non-SMTP mail systems (such as Lotus's *cc:Mail*[8]) do not separate header from envelope information. Thus, the correct addresses must appear in the header in order for the message to traverse such systems.

- A convenient way for the channel user to enter a new correspondent's channelized address into the UCDB is to simply type the full address into the To: field of the outgoing message. The PCA can then record it as it passes through untouched. Subsequent messages can be rewritten by the PCA so that the user need no longer type in the channel ID part.

## 3.3 Anomaly Detection

The PCA checks each incoming message to determine whether the sender is expected to send on the channel the message arrived on. Specifically, messages to private channels are checked to see whether the sender is a "member" of the channel. If not, the user is notified (once for a given correspondent and channel) and the event logged in the UCDB. This is not done for public channels, because one expects previously unknown correspondents to send on public channels. Channel switching anomalies are discussed in Section 4.

**User Channel Database for "hall@research.att.com"**

*Channel Map*

| Create Public | Create Private | Create SendOnly |

```
[1B8SYC8YNL]  Private OPEN (mybuddy@geewhiz.com)
[1AWTYY62HI]  Private OPEN (jrandom@j.r.isp.net)
[2BPDXY7PQ6]  Public  OPEN
[0YY4GNX8UQ]  SendOnly CLOSED
```

| Close Channel | Open Channel | Delete Channel | (select first)

*Correspondent Address Map*

| Add Corresp |

```
[1B8SYC8YNL]  mybuddy-1GG8HIAQ7N-@geewhiz.com
[1AWTYY62HI]  jrandom-1BK46WLBU2-@j.r.isp.net
```

| Delete Corresp | Switch Channel | (select first)

Figure 3: User channel database for user `hall`

### 3.4 Administrative Interface

When the user needs to open, close, create, delete, or switch channels, s/he uses the PCA's administrative interface. This interface is served by the PCA as an HTML form via HTTP. Figure 3 shows one such page. The format of a channel map listing is [<channel ID>] <class> <status> <members, if any>, while that of a correspondent-address map listing is [<channel ID>] <full address, incl. channel ID if any>. Note that closing a channel does not remove it from the UCDB; it may be reopened later. This web interface allows the PCA to be run on a machine separate from the client, so that the user's client machine need not be connected to the network in order for the PCA to carry out its processing. Moreover, existing browsers and mail clients, such as Netscape[10], work with the PCA, obviating the need for learning a new native interface. Of course, each user's administrative interface must be password protected.

## 4 Channel Switching

Occasionally, it may be desirable to switch a correspondent from one channel to another, either because the old channel has been leaked to too many adversaries, or because the user wishes to "upgrade" that correspondent's access, say from public to private or temporary to permanent. If the correspondent does not use a PCA, this requires notifying him/her to make a manual address book change. In this case, the PCA can help only in sending out a notification message.

However, if the correspondent also uses a PCA, the switching can be automated via a *channel switching protocol*. This allows the user's PCA to make a change in the correspondent-address map of the correspondent's UCDB. However, such a protocol introduces a security risk; for example, an insecure protocol might allow a PCA to be tricked into sending private messages to a public forum. This section discusses both a cryptographic protocol (most secure, but requiring key certification infrastructure) and the non-cryptographic CS-NC protocol (easy to implement, and likely secure enough) for channel switching.

Both protocols rely on each PCA establishing an *administrative channel* with a well-known channel ID, such as "2ADMINISTR". Messages on this channel will only be seen and reacted to by the PCA itself; any message on this channel not recognized as a valid administrative message will be discarded. All protocol messages discussed below are sent to and from this channel of the appropriate PCA.

## 4.1 Cryptographic Protocol

The most secure protocol requires that the user's PCA send a digitally signed channel switch message containing the new channel ID to the PCA of the correspondent, which authenticates the message, carries out the change, and then sends a digitally signed acknowledgement back to the user's PCA, so that the user's PCA knows when to close the old channel. Aside from the possibility of messages received out of order, no messages are lost this way, and a PCA cannot be tricked into changing a channel by a malicious adversary, assuming the private keys are not compromised. (The out of order message problem can be solved by keeping the old channel open for some limited time period after receipt of the acknowledgement message.) However, each party obtaining a signature key for the other is currently problematic due to the need for key certification.

## 4.2 Non-cryptographic Protocol

The PCA prototype implements an alternative, somewhat less secure protocol named CS-NC (for Channel Switching – Non-Cryptographic). The advantage of CS-NC is that it does not require cryptographic infrastructure, such as a key certification authority. Because it is less secure, CS-NC constrains the set of channel switches allowed to occur automatically, thereby limiting the possible mischief that can be caused. First, the user and host parts of the address must remain the same. This prohibits an adversary from, for example, tricking a PCA into sending private messages to an embarrassing public forum, such as a mailing list. Also, the PCA will allow channel changes only when the class indicator does not increase in magnitude. Thus, assuming the user's attention is higher for lower-numbered channel classes, the PCA will not be tricked into downgrading a correspondent so that messages might be ignored longer than expected.

To understand the security of CS-NC, it is important first to understand the threat model. Briefly, I assume no attacker is able to interdict (i.e., modify or delete in transit) a message between two legitimate endpoints. Moreover, all attackers are either eavesdroppers, capable of reading the contents of messages between two other endpoints, or non-eavesdroppers. All attackers are assumed capable of forging

CHANNELS: AVOIDING UNWANTED ELECTRONIC MAIL    95

{[C2] j–C1–@jhost, ax88jqyy9, ---}              {[C1] i–C2–@ihost, 3gu6o83wr, ---}

PCA $_i$                                         PCA $_j$

t
i
m
e

To: j-2ADMINISTR-@jhost

Key Request
i@ihost ax88jqyy9

To: i-2ADMINISTR-@ihost

Key Response
j@jhost
ax88jqyy9   3gu6o83wr

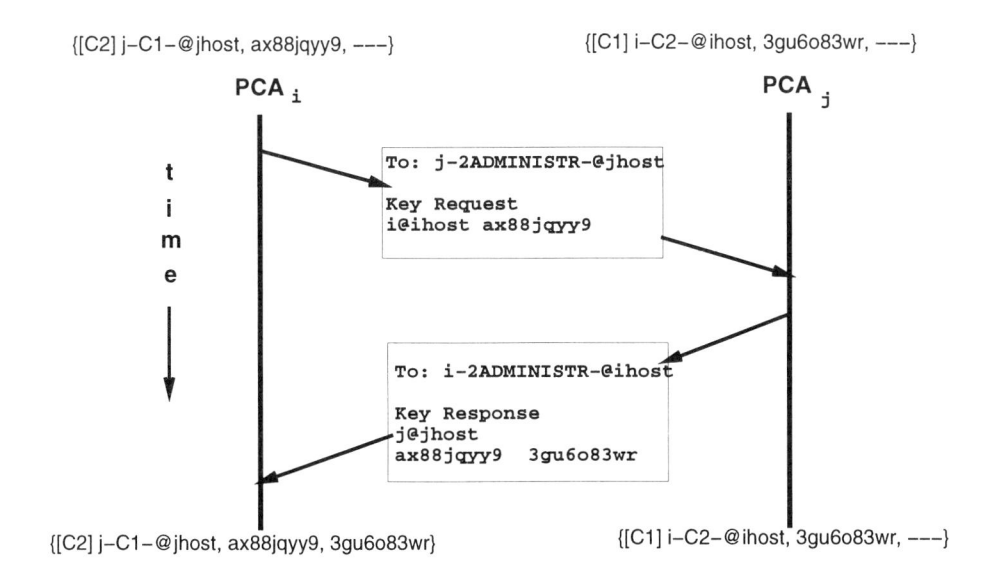

{[C2] j–C1–@jhost, ax88jqyy9, 3gu6o83wr}          {[C1] i–C2–@ihost, 3gu6o83wr, ---}

Figure 4: The messages exchanged during a key request/response interaction. Relevant portions of the UCDBs are shown in braces. After the key response is received, PCA$_i$ knows $K_j(i)$.

messages untraceably. CS-NC is designed to be secure against attacks by non-eavesdroppers; moreover, channel switches caused by eavesdroppers are detected so that the parties can be notified and action taken.

CS-NC operates in two phases. First, each PCA$_i$ creates an unguessable random key for each correspondent PCA$_j$; denote this key by $K_i(j)$. In order for PCA$_i$ to successfully switch the channel used by PCA$_j$ in PCA$_j$'s UCDB, PCA$_i$ must know $K_j(i)$. Whenever PCA$_j$ receives a *key request message* of the form

[KEY-REQUEST $i$-address $K_i(j)$]

for a user $i$ having an entry in its UCDB, it sends a *key response message* to the administrative channel of user $i$ of form:

[KEY-RESPONSE $j$-address $K_i(j)$ $K_j(i)$]

PCA$_i$ then records $K_j(i)$ in its UCDB. To obtain the key of PCA$_j$, PCA$_i$ simply sends a key request containing its own key for $j$, $K_i(j)$, and waits for the key response containing that string, ignoring any other key responses. (See Figure 4.) In this way, the two PCAs can exchange these keys and noone but eavesdroppers can obtain the keys without authorization. Note that non-eavesdropping attackers can cause extra key responses, but they cannot actually read any of them, because the responses are sent to the legitimate user's administrative address.

Now, to switch channels using the CS-NC protocol, PCA$_i$ sends a *channel switch message* containing $K_j(i)$ plus the new channel identifier to PCA$_j$. If PCA$_j$ receives

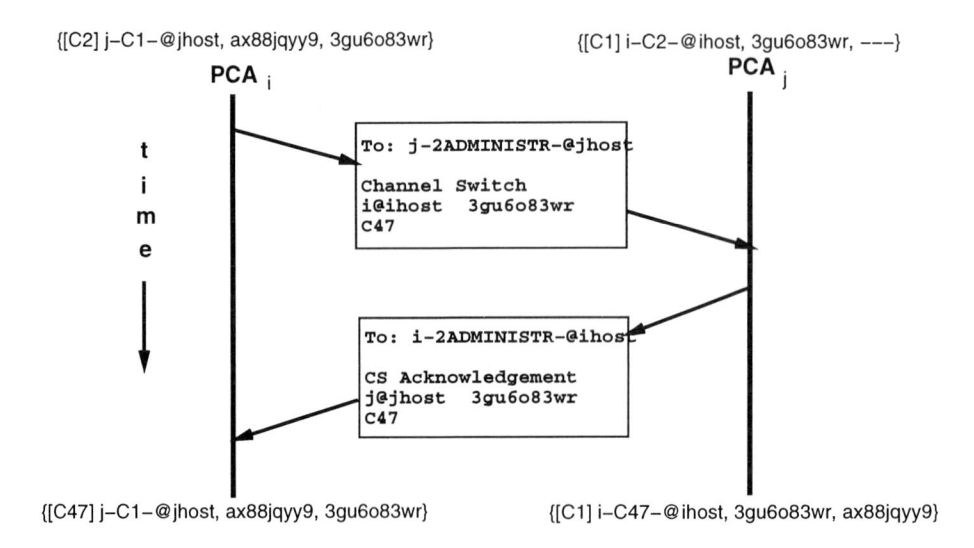

{[C2] j–C1–@jhost, ax88jqyy9, 3gu6o83wr}   {[C1] i–C2–@ihost, 3gu6o83wr, ---}

**PCA$_i$**   **PCA$_j$**

t
i
m
e

```
To: j-2ADMINISTR-@jhost

Channel Switch
i@ihost    3gu6o83wr
C47
```

```
To: i-2ADMINISTR-@ihost

CS Acknowledgement
j@jhost    3gu6o83wr
C47
```

{[C47] j–C1–@jhost, ax88jqyy9, 3gu6o83wr}   {[C1] i–C47–@ihost, 3gu6o83wr, ax88jqyy9}

Figure 5: The messages exchanged during a channel switch interaction. Relevant portions of the UCDBs are shown in braces. After sending the acknowledgement, PCA$_j$ believes C47 is $i$'s channel and also knows $K_i(j)$.

such a message containing $i$'s (unchannelized) address and $K_j(i)$, it carries out the switch and sends an *acknowledgement message* on the administrative channel back to PCA$_i$ containing $K_j(i)$ and the new channel identifier obtained from the switch message. When PCA$_i$ receives the acknowledgement with the key and channel correct, it closes the old channel. (See Figure 5.)

Whenever either PCA receives a key response, switch, or acknowledgement message not containing the correct key, it ignores it. However, when it *unexpectedly* receives either a key response or switch acknowledgement message that has the correct key, it can infer the action of an eavesdropper. A key response message would be unexpected, for example, if the PCA had sent no previous key request message. Likewise, a switch acknowledgement message would be unexpected if the PCA had sent no switch message. When a PCA infers the actions of an eavesdropper it can notify the user who can then notify the correspondent. This notification can be done outside of email (such as by phone) or else can be done automatically by an extension of these techniques using the administrative channel.

## 5 Limitations and Future Work

*Usability.* From the viewpoint of the client, a PCA makes channels transparent in everyday usage to the email user. There are, however, several occasions when extra operations must be performed, including

- When a message is to be sent to a new correspondent, that correspondent's channelized address must be entered in the to field of the email client. The

PCA then remembers the channel ID and inserts it into succeeding messages to that correspondent. The PCA also opens a new incoming channel for the correspondent.

- The user must use the administrative interface to allocate other new channels, e.g. for use in mailing lists or as temporary reply channels, or to close or switch channels.

- Malicious actions by an eavesdropper or interdicter may need to be countered by changing the security policy for a correspondent, such as by switching him/her to an authenticated channel.

I have extensively tested the prototype in a laboratory setting, and initial experience has been positive; in particular, the extra operations were relatively infrequent and have seemed easy to perform and understand. However, it is an open question whether *most* users will come to the same conclusions, particularly when used in a real-world setting rife with financially motivated adversaries. Future work will test the prototype under more realistic conditions in order to help settle this question.

*Interoperation with traditional email.* While a correspondent who does not use a PCA must directly use the user's channelized address, most mail clients provide online address books, eliminating the need to remember or type the longer address. Due to the cc and reply/forward problems, the channel ID may be leaked when the correspondent sends a multi-recipient message. Automatic channel switching is not possible, but the user's PCA can automatically generate notifications to each correspondent on the changing channel, leaving it to the correspondent to update his/her address book.

*Directories.* Any approach based on not telling everyone how to reach you appears to conflict with directories which, of course, tell everyone how to reach you. This tension results from both wanting to be reachable by people and yet not wanting to have one's time and attention wasted. Channels help resolve this tension in two ways: (1) one is more willing to publish an easily changeable address than a permanent address; and (2) when electronic money is common place, users can publish introductory channels (discussed above) in directories, thereby allowing access to legitimate correspondents but deterring unwanted correspondents financially.

*Cc asymmetry.* Note that just because user A sends a message to B and C, it is not necessarily the case that B has a channel for C or C for B. Thus, the accustomed symmetry of multi-recipient messages that allows anyone to reply to all no longer holds. However, this is desirable, since A probably does not intend to confer unlimited access to B on C or vice versa. When a stable group needs to confer with each other, either the members can simply exchange channels or else a private list can be set up by user A (see Section 2.2) that allows the group to confer yet does not give B direct access to C.

*Automatic channel switching limitations.* While I believe the channel switching protocol is secure against malicious non-eavesdroppers, and also that it reliably detects the actions of eavesdroppers, a machine-aided formal proof of these properties for an executable version of CS-NC is in progress. If messages can be *interdicted*, then the protocol is insecure and the only viable alternative is the use of cryptographic authentication. However, if one's messages can be interdicted, the adversary can do worse things than switch channels, so cryptographic privacy and authentication are probably necessary anyway. Note that even such an adversary can only switch to another, possibly closed, channel of the same user. While vulnerability to interdiction may rule out use of the non-cryptographic protocol in some situations, it is useful in others. For example, it seems unlikely messages between user accounts in a well-run online service can be interdicted or easily eavesdropped.

Note that when a user changes service provider the non-cryptographic protocol will not work, because more than the channel ID must change. Instead, the PCA can only send out standard messages to correspondents informing them of the change and inviting them to verify the change through other means. Note that the Unix .forward(5) forwarding mechanism works with channels, so mail can be forwarded to the new address during the interval immediately after the change.

*Internet telephony.* While the channels idea cannot be easily extended to the traditional telephone network, due to the fixed length and meaning of phone numbers, the approach should be usable with internet telephony (iphone)[14], since addresses can be arbitrarily long. The approach should even work when accessing iphone service from a standard telephone set, as long as the call is placed via a server running a PCA that could translate the input phone number or nickname into a channelized iphone address. Administration could either be via a web interface or, perhaps, automatic speech recognition.

# 6 Other Approaches

The idea of augmenting the user name portion of an email address with information to aid in routing is not new. The Andrew mail system[2] uses addresses of the form user+info@host, where info is an arbitrary alphanumeric field. Each user may write code in the FLAMES language to process messages based in part on the contents of the info field. While the Andrew system could be used to implement the channels approach, it has not been used in that way. Instead, it has been up to the good will of correspondents not to purposely miscategorize messages, e.g. by sending junk mail advertisements to user+urgent@host. Such a system, with well-known or easily guessable "channels", cannot stand up to the likely onslaught of unwanted email in a commercial world.

*Kill files.* Another way to avoid email is to automatically discard all messages from a user, site, or even domain. This approach unfairly denies access to legitimate users at the site or domain, and is easily evaded through forgery or by having multiple addresses. With channels, it is possible to grant access to any set of individuals, denying access to others, and forgery does not help an adversary evade the channel mechanism.

*Email agents and filtering.* Email filtering agents[6, 2] can be used to discard messages that fail to satisfy user-defined criteria. However, it is extremely difficult to define syntactic rules that reliably distinguish advertisements and surveys from legitimate messages. User-written rule sets are doomed to lose an "arms race" against clever human junk mailers. Consider the following message, excerpted from one I received recently after purchasing software from the company who makes software package Y:

```
From: frobboz@somewhere.edu (Chuck Frobboz)
To: hall@research.att.com
Subject: Difficulty using <sw package X>

Dear Robert,
I have difficulty using <sw package X> with JR WordProcessor.
[...exposition of some problem...]
Isn't this frustrating?  Maybe you would like to check out
<sw package Y>.  It is really cool.  Here is the URL:[...]

-- Chuck
```

I read several lists where people describe legitimate problems in using software packages. This message, really an advertisement, is so similar in form and content to those that it would be extremely difficult to write an email filter that reliably discards this message but lets through legitimate ones. On the other hand, if this arrived on a channel allocated to commercial firms, it would have been easy to spot; in fact, a PCA could even demand e-money in advance for a slice of the user's attention.

*Cryptographic authentication.* One can enforce access control by requiring all messages to be digitally signed by an authorized correspondent; the cryptographic filter would discard any other messages. If available, this is an alternative to private channels when messages come from known correspondents, providing good protection against unauthorized messages; however, even though software packages exist to do the cryptographic operations[5, 12], reliably obtaining the public key of a correspondent is still problematic[13]. Even if this were solved, there is still the major question of how to deal with messages from unknown correspondents, such as are received from mailing lists. Even if a message is digitally signed with a certified key, it does not guarantee the message is not junk. One can accumulate a (large) list of individuals who send junk, but adversaries can evade this mechanism by registering several addresses and keys, or by having a different employee send each message. Channels, on the other hand, allow one to absolutely shut off the flow of messages from an adversary by closing all channels known to it. To gain unauthorized access, s/he must invest effort, risk, or money in eavesdropping or social engineering, while the new access can be easily cut off once again after just one message. Thus, defeating channels is economically unfavorable to the adversary.

*Cookies in headers.* A slight variation of the channels idea is instead of changing the address, require an appropriate channel ID in some other field of the message header. While viable for one-to-one messages, this fails to handle mailing lists: each contributor to the list would have to include channel IDs for all recipients, an impossible task. Of course, a sophisticated list manager could solve this by storing the appropriate channel ID for each address subscribed and making a tailored copy of each message for each recipient. Unfortunately, no existing list servers work this way; putting the channel ID in the address allows the channels approach to interoperate with all existing list servers.

*Legislation.* One might consider extending existing laws governing junk physical mail and telemarketing calls to cover email as well; however, the global Internet is not governed by a single jurisdiction. Also, legislation would presumably only be effective against law-abiding junk-mailers and not harassers and other undesirables.

## 7 Conclusion

If people don't know your address, they can't send you email. The channels approach exploits this idea, providing a simple yet effective way to avoid unwanted email. The personal channel agent can automate essentially all of the operations necessary to managing the complexities introduced by channels, so that typical daily use will be transparent to email users. Channels complement cryptographic authentication, because channels give control over messages received from unknown correspondents such as advertisers, survey takers, harassers, and mailing list contributors. In a time of increasing commercialism and decreasing individual privacy, I believe the channels approach shows promise and should be pursued.

**Acknowledgement.** Thanks to Greg Blonder for discussions and comments.

## References

[1] L. Blum, M. Blum & M. Shub; A simple unpredictable pseudo-random number generator; *SIAM J. Comput. v.15(2)*, 364–383; SIAM, 1986.

[2] N. Borenstein & C. Thyberg; Power, ease of use, and cooperative work in a practical multimedia message system; *Intl. J. Man-Machine Studies, 34*, April, 1991.

[3] B. Costales, E. Allman, & N. Rickert; *Sendmail*; Sebastopol, CA: O'Reilly and Assoc; 1993.

[4] R. Fielding, J.Gettys, J.Mogul, H.Frystyk, T.Berners-Lee; Hypertext Transfer Protocol – HTTP/1.1 (work in progress); June 7, 1996; http://www.w3.org/pub/WWW/Protocols/HTTP/Issues/Revs/Rev87Clean.txt

[5] S. Garfinkel; *PGP: Pretty Good Privacy*; Sebastopol, CA: O'Reilly and Assoc; 1995.

[6] I. Greif; Desktop agents in group-enabled products; *Comm. ACM, 37(7)*, July 1994.

[7] M. Hannah; HTML Reference Manual; Sandia National Laboratories, 1996; http://www.sandia.gov/sci_compute/html_ref.html.

[8] Lotus *cc:Mail*; http://www.lotus.com/comms/ccmail.htm

[9] J. Myers & M. Rose; "Post Office Protocol – Version 3"; Network Working Group Request for Comments 1725 (RFC 1725, November 1994); http://andrew2.andrew.cmu.edu/rfc/rfc1725.

[10] Netscape Communications Corp; *Netscape Navigator, v2.0 (or later)*; http://home.netscape.com.

[11] J. Postel; Simple mail transfer protocol; Internet RFC 821, 1982. http://www.cis.ohio-state.edu/htbin/rfc/rfc821.html

[12] RSA Data Security; All about S/MIME; http://www.rsa.com/rsa/ S-MIME/

[13] B. Schneier; *Applied Cryptography, 2nd ed*; New York, NY: Wiley; 1996.

[14] Vocaltec; "Welcome to Vocaltec: The Internet Phone Company"; http://www.vocaltec.com.

AT&T LABS RESEARCH, 180 PARK AVE, RM A033, FLORHAM PARK, NJ 07932.

*Email address:* hall@research.att.com

# Demonstration of Hacker Techniques

## Cynthia D. Cullen

Abstract: This is a summary of a demonstration at the DIMACS Workshop on Network Threats. The intent of this demonstration is to educate users, system administrators, and security personnel. Demonstrations of security vulnerabilities make everyone aware of the risks involved. Three hacker tools ypgrab, rootkit and ttywatcher were demonstrated. These tools have been available within the hacker community for several years and are available on the Internet.

## 1. Introduction

Hacker tools exist for attacking most network protocols (e.g., TCP/IP, IPX, etc.). The tools demonstrated, at the conference, work against TCP/IP networks. These tools consist of tools expressly designed and developed for hacking existing applications/operating systems and system administrator tools. For example, simple network management protocol (SNMP) applications, such as cmu-snmp, obtain information. Often network administrators do not change default SNMP community strings (passwords). Hackers use these to obtain hardware, operating system, and routing information.

The intent of the demonstration is to show users, systems administrators, and security personnel how a hacker compromises a system.

1991 Mathematics Subject Classifications. Primary 68-06; Secondary 68N99

## 2. The Tools

Hacker tools are constantly evolving. New tools are being developed and existing ones modified. Often the modifications are not enhancements. The user does not fully understand the functionality of the tool being modified. Modifications of complex tools like rootkit — where the commands are interdependent — are expected. Tracking of tool distribution and hacker collaboration occurs via these modifications.

Three hacker tools were demonstrated: rootkit, ttywatcher, and ypgrab. Each of these programs has been around in the hacker community for an extended period of time. With these tools it is possible to go from no authorized access to controlling the system and the network.

The general idea is to use ypgrab to gain access to a system. Then, obtain root (administrative) access and install rootkit on the compromised system. Finally, use ttywatcher to compromise networked systems and the network.

### 2.1 *ypgrab*

*ypgrab* lists the contents of NIS (Network Information System) tables. The main target (also the default) is the password table. *ypgrab* requires the domain name to gain access to the NIS tables. Often the domain name is easy to guess. NIS password files usually contain hundreds of entries. Once obtained, a password cracker program is run against the passwords. If even one of the passwords is cracked (successfully guessed), access is gained to all systems in that NIS domain. One of a multitude of security weaknesses is exploited to obtain root on the NIS servers, slaves or any of the clients. One way is to look for *root* accounts. Root access may be available for owners of the NIS client workstations via *sudo* or rUID accounts. *sudo* is a public domain program for managing root access to systems. *sudo* controls exactly which commands a user can run as root and to audit what a user has done as root. However the control and audit functions do not work if the user can run shells (*ksh, bsh, sh*, etc).

rUID accounts provide local user's root privileges for their system only. rUID accounts are located in the NIS client workstation's /etc/password file. When one NIS account is compromised, it is used to obtain all the local password files. These are searched for the rUID accounts.

### 2.2 Rootkit

The hacker installs rootkit after obtaining root access. Rootkit maintains control of a compromised system and hides the existence of the hacker.

Rootkit initially was only available to an elite group of hackers. It is a comprehensive set of programs that includes a makefile and documentation. Once installed it is difficult to detect the hacker. The standard commands used to quickly review a system for problems does not reveal the hacker. Rootkit has the following effects:
- removes entries from the utmp, wtmp and lastlog file;
- the ls and du commands are modified to hide files;
- the ps command does not show the hacker's processes;
- ifconfig does not show the network interface to be in PROMISC mode;

# DEMONSTRATION OF HACKER TECHNIQUES

- a root backdoor is installed into the login program;
- checksums, installation dates and modification dates appear to be the same as original files.

Typically rootkit contains the following program replacements:

z2: As root execute "z2 login" (where "login" is the id you want erased). The login specified will be erased from utmp, wtmp, and lastlog.

es: As root execute *es*. This will open the system's network interface in promiscuous mode and will monitor all the TCP/IP traffic being broadcasted to that portion of the network. *es* looks at all telnet, rlogin, smtp and ftp connections and records the IP address of the originating and destination systems and the logins and passwords used to establish the connection. *es* has the following options: -b (create a background process), -d (debug), -i (specify network interface) and -f (filename for output).

fix: Fix attempts to fake checksums and installs the "rootkit" programs with the same date, permissions, user name and group name as the original system files/programs.

sl: Sl is a modified *login* program with a hardcoded password installed. The magic password grants access for all valid logins on the system (e.g., root). (Note: running *strings* on the *sl* binary/executable does not display the magic password, due to the way the buffer is loaded.)

ic: When *ifconfig* is replaced with *ic*, it will remove the "PROMISC" portion in the output when the network interface is in promiscuous mode (e.g., when *es* is running). The "PROMISC" portion of *ifconfig* output
 warns the system administrator when someone is monitoring network traffic via the network interface device.

ps: The modified *ps* allows an intruder to strip out uids, ptys, ttys or commands currently in the process list; the modified *ps* does not modify the process list. The uids, ptys, ttys and/or commands that are to be stripped extracted from a file specified by rootkit.

ns: The modified *netstat* (*ns*) program allows an intruder to strip specific network connections from the network listing. The actual interface is not modified only the output of the *netstat* program.

ls and ls5: Ls and ls5 are modified *ls* (listing) programs that allow an intruder to hide the existence of files and directories. A sample file follows:

```
rootkit.shar    # Don't show file rootkit.shar
rookit.d        # Don't show directory   rootkit.d
ptyr            # Don't show file ptyr (this file!)
```

du and du5: *du* and *du5* are modified *du* (disk usage) programs that allow an intruder to display the disk blocks (per directory) minus the disk blocks being used by the intruder's files and directories. (the same as *ls* and *ls5*).

Even experienced system administrator have a hard time detecting a rootkit infestation if they are not familiar with it. A simple check is to import a clean copy of *ls* from OS distribution media. Check the checksum, size, and time stamp on the above mentioned programs.

### 2.3 *ttywatcher*

Once one system is compromised, *ttywatcher* can be used to compromise other systems on the network. Any system that connects to or is connected to the compromised system, via tty's, is vulnerable. *ttywatcher* provides a GUI interface that shows all active ttys. The intruder has multiple options with *ttywatcher*:

- A session may be taken over for a short period of time, the network appears slow to the session originator.
- A session can be taken over permanently, the session appears hung to the user.
- A session can be "piggybacked" (e.g., shared between the hijacker and the session originator.) In this situation the session originator sees all commands typed by the hijacker.
- A session can be monitored. When a user logins into another system, the password can be observed. If the user becomes root on another system that password is visible.
- Single, multiple or all sessions can be terminated.

**Figure 1** Ttywatcher's GUI Interface.

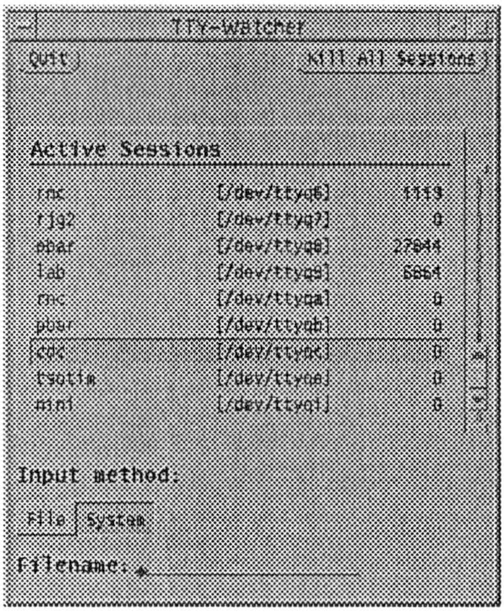

*ttywatcher* is an especially dangerous tool because it can be used to get around firewalls and authentication mechanisms. Suppose a user logs into the corporate network via a compromised terminal provided at a conference. Assume the corporation has a firewall and a one-time authentication mechanism (e.g., Bellcore's S/Key, Digital Pathway's Defender, or Security Dynamic's SecurID) in place. The firewall allows e-mail, DNS, and strongly authenticated telnet traffic in and all traffic out of the network. The user telnets to a server, authenticates and is given access. Now the hacker has access to the internal corporate network via ttywatcher. The strong authentication mechanism is bypassed by having a legitimate user authenticate prior to taking over the session.

The strong authentication mechanism prevent direct access into the network. However, scripts can be installed where access is initiated from within the corporate network. For example, a script run out of cron displays a X-windows xterm window on the hackers workstation periodically (e.g., every Wednesday at 11pm). The hacker probes the rest of the internal corporate network for security vulnerabilities looking for root access. Once root access is obtained, the whole network is compromised.

Figure 2: Ttywatcher window monitoring a tty.

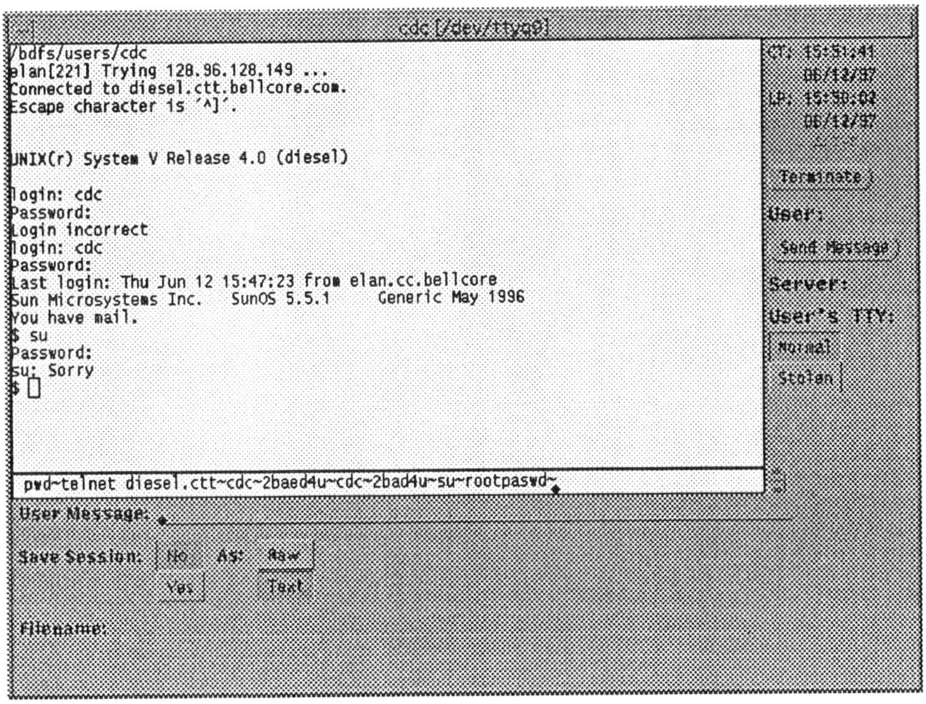

As the name implies, ttywatcher works only with sessions requiring a tty. It does not work on UDP traffic. All ttys — both incoming and outgoing connections — can be monitored. Typically, telnet and rlogin traffic are monitored. Rsh traffic cannot be monitor because no tty is used.

Ttywatcher has a GUI interface (Figure 1). All active sessions are listed in the window. If the hacker wants to terminate all sessions, simply push the *Kill All Sessions* button in the upper right hand corner. The hacker inputs a script by specifying the *filename* and pushing the *file* button. A single click on an active session pops up the screen shown if Figure 2. The white screen in figure 2 shows the data that is displayed on the user's terminal. The single line at the bottom on the white screen ("pwd~telnet diesel.ctt") contains the keystrokes of the user. The ~ are return characters. In this example the user ran the command pwd, then *telnet*'ed to system diesel.ctt. The user mis-typed the password as 2baed4u, then log into diesel with password 2bad4u. Then, the use attempted to *su* to root with a password of *rootpasswd*. She is denied root access. The user sees all commands the hacker is typing when the *Normal* button is pushed. The hacker pushes the *Stolen* button to hide commands from the user. After inputting commands the hacker returns the session to the user by pushing the *Normal* button. The *Terminate* button on the right side of figure 2 terminates that particular session.

## 2.4 Summary

These three tools — *ypgrab*, rootkit, and *ttywatcher* — are examples of how an intruder, who has access to your network, goes from no authorized access to total control of the network. *ypgrab* and rootkit are hacker tools by design. *ttywatcher* is an administrative tools that is being used by hackers to monitor and hijack sessions.

### APPENDEX A
**Following are the release notes from rootkit.**
------------------
rootkit release 1.
------------------
After spending tons of time having to do all of this by myself, I finally decided to write a simple makefile to do it for me. Call me a script cracker, but I'm lazy as hell. You don't want to use it, you don't have to. Keep in mind it takes me a max of 40 seconds on a 4/65 to compile and install every program here. Can you beat that by hand? :-)
Here is how it works:
execute the command: ' make all install ' The following programs will be installed suid root in DESTDIR:

z2: removes entries from utmp, wtmp, and lastlog.
es: rokstar's ethernet sniffer for sun4 based kernels.
fix: try to fake checksums, install with same dates/perms/u/g.

note:   if you do not want these files installed suid (the administrator has a cron to check for suid files, or the like), then type make cleansuid and the suid bits will be removed.

The following programs will be patched and an attempt at spoofing the checksums of the files will be made. Also, these files will be installed with the same dates, permissions, owners, and groups of the originals.

sl: become root via a magic password sent to login.
ic: modified ifconfig to remove PROMISC flag from output.
ps:
ns:
ls:
du5:
ls5:

Here are some notes on the patch for 'ps':

1. This doesn't modify the process lists, so your processes are STILL in memory, but ps just won't administrator has another copy of ps sitting on Best to search for SGID kmem programs to be fairly sure.

2. An example /dev/ptyp file is as follows:

| 0 0 | Strips all processes running under | root |
| 1 p0 | Strips tty p0 | |
| 2 sniffer | Strips all programs with | the name sniffer |

3. Do not leave a NULL string anywhere in the file. During testing, I often pressed return after my last control statement. Do not do this as it will cause a meory fault. Do not use a character as the first line in the control file Remember to convert the UID's you wished masked to thier numerical format.

4. Programs such as "top" will still show processes running This is bad. I'm working on a patch.

Here are some notes on the patch for 'netstat':

1. This doesn't modify network listings, so your network connections are STILL in memory, but 'netstat' just won't display them. If another copy of 'netstat' is run on the machine, it will produce accurate results.
   Best to search for SGID kmem programs to be fairly sure.

2. An example /dev/ptyq file is as follows:

| 0 6667 | # Strip all foreign irc network | connections |
| 1 23 | # Strip all local telnet | connections |
| 2 .209.5 | # Strip all foreign connections | from cert.org |

3.175.9.8     # Strip all local connections to         netsys4.netsys.com

3. Do not leave a NULL string anywhere in the file. It will cause a memory fault. When stripping addresses, a string search is used to compare addresses in the control file with actaul network connections. This could cause minor problems.

4. It would probably be better to only strip the address ONCE for each line in the control file. Adding such commands is trivial. Check 'inet.c' for modifications.

Here are some notes on the patch for 'ls' && 'du' && 'du5' && 'ls5':

1. ls and du are trojaned and your files will not be listed unless you issue a / flag.

2. Example /dev/ptyr
sunsnif        # Strip the filename sunsnif
icmpfake       # Strip the filename icmpfake

3. Would be useful if stripping uids, and gids was included.
----
later eleetz, have fun and don't fuq shit up, all it duz iz get people put in jail. werd.

Cynthia D. Cullen is a Principal Consultant at Bell Communications Research. She can be reached at ccullen@notes.cc.bellcore.com

# Selected Titles in This Series
(*Continued from the front of this publication*)

9 **William T. Trotter, Editor,** Planar Graphs

8 **Simon Gindikin, Editor,** Mathematical Methods of Analysis of Biopolymer Sequences

7 **Lyle A. McGeoch and Daniel D. Sleator, Editors,** On-Line Algorithms

6 **Jacob E. Goodman, Richard Pollack, and William Steiger, Editors,** Discrete and Computational Geometry: Papers from the DIMACS Special Year

5 **Frank Hwang, Fred Roberts, and Clyde Monma, Editors,** Reliability of Computer and Communication Networks

4 **Peter Gritzmann and Bernd Sturmfels, Editors,** Applied Geometry and Discrete Mathematics, The Victor Klee Festschrift

3 **E. M. Clarke and R. P. Kurshan, Editors,** Computer-Aided Verification '90

2 **Joan Feigenbaum and Michael Merritt, Editors,** Distributed Computing and Cryptography

1 **William Cook and Paul D. Seymour, Editors,** Polyhedral Combinatorics